Richard Vander Vaart's triumph of memory is a collection of precious pieces for all the rest of us. Through stories that are honest and overflowing with the reality of the life and ministry of a young pastor, we laugh, we cry, we are stirred, and we pray. Through stories that are precious in their specificity, we are led with certainty to biblical grounding and theological reflection. The stories may be specific but they speak to us all. They reverberate both with the depths of our humanity and the awesome reality of the grace and glory of God.

Thanks be to God for memory and the ability to express it in ways that strengthen and inspire.

—*The Rev. Dr. Karen Hamilton,*
The Canadian Council of Churches General Secretary

•— FOLLOWING THE SHEPHERD IN REAL LIFE —•

Can't Help Myself

*Short stories and
daily devotions*

RICHARD T. VANDER VAART
Photographer Marianne VanderSpek

CAN'T HELP MYSELF
Copyright © 2016 by Richard T. Vander Vaart
Photography by Marianne VanderSpek

All rights reserved. Neither this publication nor any part of this publication may be reproduced or transmitted in any form or by any means, electronic or mechanical, including photocopying, recording or any information storage and retrieval system, without permission in writing from the author.

Scripture quotations are taken from the Holy Bible, New Living Translation, copyright ©1996, 2004, 2007, 2013, 2015 by Tyndale House Foundation. Used by permission of Tyndale House Publishers, Inc., Carol Stream, Illinois 60188. All rights reserved. Scripture quotations marked (NIV) are taken from the Holy Bible, New International Version®, NIV®. Copyright © 1973, 1978, 1984, 2011 by Biblica, Inc.™ Used by permission of Zondervan. All rights reserved worldwide. The "NIV" and "New International Version" are trademarks registered in the United States Patent and Trademark Office by Biblica, Inc.™ Scripture quotations marked (KJV) taken from the Holy Bible, King James Version, which is in the public domain.

Printed in Canada

ISBN: 978-1-4866-1304-5

Word Alive Press
131 Cordite Road, Winnipeg, MB R3W 1S1
www.wordalivepress.ca

Library and Archives Canada Cataloguing in Publication

Vander Vaart, Richard T., 1963-, author
    Can't help myself : short stories and daily devotions / Richard T. Vander Vaart.

Issued in print and electronic formats.
ISBN 978-1-4866-1304-5 (paperback).--ISBN 978-1-4866-1305-2 (ebook)

    1. Clergy--Anecdotes. 2. Christian life--Anecdotes. 3. Reformed Church--Prayers and devotions. I. Title.

FOREWORD

Jesus called out to them, "Come, follow me, and I will show you how to fish for people!" (Matthew 4:19)

Then Jesus came to them and said, "All authority in heaven and on earth has been given to me. Therefore go and make disciples of all nations, baptizing them in the name of the Father and of the Son and of the Holy Spirit, and teaching them to obey everything I have commanded you. And surely I am with you always, to the very end of the age." (Matthew 28:18–20)

FROM THE BEGINNING OF CHRIST'S MINISTRY TO THE TIME OF THE GREAT commission only a moment before His ascension, the disciples' response to Him has always been proclaiming the gospel and making more disciples.

Unfortunately, many of today's Christians have diluted discipleship to a nonchalant "God bless you! I will pray for you. See you next Sunday!" We forget that Jesus was intimately involved in the lives of His disciples as they followed Him.

If we were to look at most of the parables from His teachings, we'd find they are stories based on the agricultural life that was intimately familiar to His original first-century audience. Some aspects of unfamiliar concepts, such as the kingdom of God, were compared to something from everyday life that could easily be understood.

And the shortest verse in the Bible is John 11:35: *"Jesus wept."* A Christ who can't weep is not the Christ who knows the joy and sorrows we know so well. Christ was the best example of a disciple-maker not only because He was God, but because He was also a man who was involved in the lives of those around Him. He related His divine knowledge to His surroundings and taught from it. He walked with His disciples, shared His story, and accepted theirs.

When Richard and I first met in the winter of 2015, he thought I was unteachable, and I thought I did not need to be taught; we were not enemies, but we also were not friends. Obviously, the fact that I'm writing his first book's foreword is proof that we were both wrong.

A few months after we met, in the early summer of that year, he and his wife moved to St. Thomas, Ontario. We ended up serving in the same church. He was new to the city and I was wading through the murky water of ministry, direly in need of a mentor who would not withhold his comments. And by the grace of God, he has not withheld anything, but instead embodied Proverbs 27:17 to a profound degree: *"As iron sharpens iron, so one person sharpens another."*

If you know the Reverend Richard Vander Vaart, you know that his Christ-like discipleship attitude has a tendency to captivate your attention. He will always point you to the Rock that is higher than us. He is always transparent in his walk with people around him: the blessings and struggles, joys and sorrows, even when every emotion seems so flat to him. He has a way of seeing grace in every situation—ministry life, social interactions, or a weird mushroom on the side of the street.

The stories behind the book you are holding in your hands right now were written with Richard's own humour, and tears from his ragged memories. This book will show you the world of ministry from a ministerial perspective. It portrays the lives of those on whom the Lord causes the sun to rise, and on whom He sends rain for all their seasons. The devotionals and scriptures will show you how the grace of God can be related to even the mundane things in people's lives.

For someone like me, who is in the early years of ministry and also an immigrant, this book has shown the reality of those whom the

Lord calls—and the reality that we are all citizens of heaven migrating through this world. I prayerfully hope that this book will affect your life according to the riches of Christ's abounding grace.

—James Issara

INTRODUCTION

WHY WRITE A BOOK LIKE THIS? IT'S A GOOD QUESTION. FOR ME, IT REPRESENTS A triumph of memory.

A little over a year ago, some friends were celebrating their anniversary and they recalled how my wife Carolyn and I had hosted a reception for them. Honestly, I remember this couple as dear friends and I know we have a long shared history, but so much is blank. Even as they provided specific details of the event, I couldn't bring it to mind, at all.

After being in a car accident on January 5, 2009, I realized I was not at home in my own brain anymore. Many memories were robbed from me, jolted, or just beyond my perception. My children would recall events and I would know we had been there—sometimes there was even pictorial evidence—but I could not shake loose the memory. At other times, I know in the past—my pre-accident past—I would respond to something with laughter, but instead tears now spring to my eyes; my emotions have been jumbled in ways I can't explain. Other times I know and feel that a moment in time is particularly significant, but my heart and mind have gone flat and I have no way of assigning the appropriate mix of emotions. It is not who I am, or who I was, or how I remember myself. I am often an observing stranger to my own past. It is so hard to explain.

In 2014, I took a leave of absence from my parish and little snippets of stories appeared—not fully formed, but shards and pieces and cherished fragments. For someone who has forgotten so much, I can't tell you how precious each piece is. I wrote some of these down. As I worked on this project, with more time on my hands than a person in full-time ministry might have for such a venture, my friends and children would say, "When you're done with this, can I have a copy?"

Please understand that some of the stories have been altered to protect the identities of those who are part of them. Some of the stories are amalgamations of various incidents and (might) have grown taller in the retelling. The names which I use in these short stories are names I have assigned for clarity.

But here it is. This book is all the more precious to me because God has given back, unexpectedly after four-plus years, more memories than I ever expected. Thanks be to His Name.

—Richard T. Vander Vaart
January 2, 2016

DECEMBER 1

Cards

ABE ADMITTED, WITH A HALF-SMILE AND SPARKLING EYES, THAT HE SOMETIMES cheated. If he wasn't caught, it didn't quite count. It was odd to be playing cards together; Abe and I had a rocky start to our friendship.

You see, as a young pastor with a young family, the house needed a lot of furnishing and our three growing children needed many clothes. Abe's contribution was heavy red velvet curtains that fit into the living room. The heavy curtains were needed to block out the stiff winter wind which was only slightly slowed by the huge window. The cracks around the frame of the window and the caulking made the curtains dance.

The worst part about the curtains was their white, plasticized backing. These old curtains would shed white plastic flakes like dandruff with each flutter of wind. When the sun was warm during the day, they would stick to the windowsill and the plastic would form a sort of glue that would peel the paint right off the sill. It was hopeless.

When confronted with all the inadequacies of this "gift," Abe was quite angry.

After church, he would huff past the line of people queued up to shake hands with their pastor. And Abe's long-suffering wife, Tina, would wait patiently, until her turn came. She'd offer a slight shrug for his antics and warmly shake my hand and thank me for the sermon, or the clever paragraph in the bulletin, or the chosen songs that had particularly moved her. There was always something, a little tidbit to soften the blowing winds of her husband's temper.

When the line dwindled and the last of the parishioners had passed by and offered their smorgasbord of comments and critiques and veiled hostilities and kindly meant correctives to their young new pastor, I'd go outside for a smoke.

Of course, there would be my angry old friend, Abe. It would be just too rude not to nod when I was near him, smoking. So a simple nod had to suffice and we'd half-turn away and smoke in semi-awkward privacy.

One day, for a reason I still can't fathom, I remember asking Tina if she played cards. In fact, she replied that she and Abe both loved playing cards. She offered the information that they were free on Saturday evening and would come by after supper when our kids were in bed.

After a long week of uncertain anticipation, it was 7:47 p.m. on Saturday. The doorbell rang. Oddly, tucked under her arm was a dark bottle. Once coats had been properly hung up and the men's stiff-legged bristling had melted away because of the women's hurried suggestions of coffee and a nice *gebakkje* (Dutch pastry). She said that after the coffee but before the cards, we'd all need a good sop of sherry; it would lighten the mood and make the cards so much more fun.

My wife caught my eye and slightly raised a questioning eyebrow. Really? We had pegged them for teetotallers, and maybe a beer on a hot summer's day, but sherry? We gulped the coffee rather quickly because it took the combined efforts of two women and all their skills to keep the conversation rolling along. Finally, glasses were produced, alcohol poured, and the cards laid out.

From the first hand, the conversation started. The rules needed to be explained and the exceptions observed. Abe would toss in the odd funny recap of incidents which had happened when they'd played with other friends. Before long, it was getting late; in fact, it was getting to be Sunday morning, the day of church. The final hand was played—and he won. He gloated terribly. He snapped his fingers and excitedly brushed back the few strands of hair that clung to his scalp.

The following morning, Abe and Tina slept in a bit later than usual. Their morning rituals had been disrupted. Long retired, they had fixed and established routines, and messing them up by sleeping in caused a kafuffle. They didn't have enough time to eat at their usual leisurely pace, with a second round of coffees, and still get dressed on time. He hurriedly drank down one coffee, chewed a piece of toast, threw on the same shirt from the night before, and added a jacket.

After the morning church service finished, he hurried downstairs to the hall where he could grab a coffee. Once more, he needled his card-playing opponents from the previous evening. Just as one rival approached, he slapped his left breast pocket; it was the habit of a smoker who'd neglected his usual routine for a round of gloating.

After the slap, his mouth dropped open. To his own embarrassment and his card-playing foe's glee, he pulled out the second hand of cards which he hadn't in fact played the previous evening. The game had gotten so intense that they'd called a brief truce and endured the bitter cold for a quick smoke. In order to keep his hand from his prying opponents, he had put this second hand of cards into the breast pocket of his dress shirt. After removing their coats and getting settled in once again, receiving another round of sherry to warm up, he forgot about the cards in his shirt; since they were not on the table at his right, where they usually were, he assumed he'd been playing his second hand instead of completing his first hand of cards.

He'd been caught.

Abe laughed at the memory. It was a great story and the relationship between us began to thaw. On Sunday, after our card game, I saw him in the smoking section, and after our usual nod I smiled and asked casually, "Did you check your shirt pocket this morning?"

Sometimes we are so familiar with the seemingly little things we do wrong. They become fodder for poking fun at our good friends. We call them foibles, but the word reminds us of the incredible force of temptations and the destruction these temptations can bring. Read on.

Return, O Israel, to the LORD your God, for your sins have brought you down. Bring your confessions, and return to the Lord. Say to him, "Forgive all our sins and graciously receive us, so that we may offer you our praises..." The LORD says, "...O Israel, stay away from idols! I am the one who answers your prayers and cares for you." (Hosea 14:1–2, 4, 8)

After doing with the dishes with me, Tanya emptied our kitchen garbage container. I kinda raised my eyebrows. Not that I didn't appreciate the help, but it was just a bit odd. We were totally comfortable with one another and Tanya and Mark weren't guests in our home; they were family.

Tanya noticed the reaction and smiled. "Our little dog wants to eat the meat scraps out of the garbage, and I'm just removing any temptation. I know he wants to be good, but the smell of the meat is too tempting for him."

That's a great image for our walk with God. We want to be good. Our sins bring us down. Temptations swirl all around us. A wise mentor, a strong Christian friend, and a faithful peer can steer us away from temptation.

Yesterday I heard a preacher say, "If you are heading to Sarnia when you intend to go to London, you can feel bad all you want, but that won't make any difference. Instead you need to turn the car around and go in the correct direction."

A good Christian friend can help us turn away from our sins. In a Christian community, we can help one another steer far from even the smallest taste of temptation so we can walk in praise to the God who answers prayer and cares for us.

> BLESS and sanctify my soul with Thy heavenly blessings, that it may become Thy holy habitation, and let nothing be found in this temple of Thy Divinity, which shall offend the eyes of Thy Majesty. According to the greatness of Thy goodness and multitude of Thy mercies, look upon me, and hear the prayer of Thy poor servant. Protect and keep my soul, amidst so many

dangers of this life, and, by Thy grace accompanying me, direct it along the way of peace to its home of everlasting brightness—Amen.

—Thomas À Kempis (1379–1471)

DECEMBER 2

This Is God

STRAIGHT AFTER GRADUATION AT SEMINARY, I DIDN'T HAVE A JOB AND I WASN'T built for landscaping (which is what a few of our peers were going to do until a pastoral charge could be found). So I contacted a few congregations that had hoped to have seminary students on summer assignments but had been unsuccessful in their search. One of the churches agreed they'd appreciate having a summer pulpit supply. That is how we found ourselves all packed up and driving the many-days-long trip from Grand Rapids, Michigan to Saskatchewan.

The drive through Chicago was madness. We were thoroughly unprepared for the onslaught of late-night traffic, tolls, and the possibility of being separated. The idea was to drive as a convoy of three vehicles and get to Wisconsin to stay at a friend's house. This friend was the lead driver... and I still remember with stomach-wrenching freshness the horror of realizing we were following her but had no address, no phone number, not even a designated meeting spot if we got separated. This was twenty-plus years ago, long before everyone and his cat had a cell phone and could text, Facebook message, or call from any location on the planet. Here we were, hurtling through the crush of toll booth traffic, and me fumbling for change while trying to see where the other two vehicles were going and all the while swallowing back the sickness creeping up my throat because I hate driving highways.

Next to me, oblivious, was our chatty almost four-year-old son, Adrian. He found the lights, traffic, and noises worthy of constant comment. At one point I was almost going to yell in frustration. I had so much going on that I was starting to lose my nerve driving this long, unfamiliar moving van. Adrian noticed the tensing muscles and twitching motions of my face and his stream of words slowed to a trickle.

Suddenly I realized what a soothing presence Adrian's words were. The less he spoke, the more the traffic affected and intimidated me. So, as gently as I could under those circumstances, I asked him a question or two about the scene painted on the moving van keeping pace with us. Happily he launched again into a detailed description of big cows—no, buffalos—and people hunting them across a huge field. He calmed me as I desperately searched among the red taillights ahead for a vehicle that was evenly slightly familiar. What if we lost one another?

Adrian kept up the wonderful tapestry of words which drove away my fears. This dad had to protect his son and his family and get into a headspace that would allow me to focus on finding the other members of our little convoy. What a joyful reunion it was when we all stopped at the same rest stop and got our final directions to our first destination.

The ordination took place on October 26 and my in-laws came out to witness this crowning celebration of four years of study. It was a morning of biting cold and there'd been fog, which settled on branches and twigs and froze as layers of frost. Everything was starkly outlined in frost and ice. The hoarfrost was brittle and beautiful.

The little church was packed full, and as I knelt and received the laying on of hands, a seed of peace settled into my heart—a seed of peace nurtured by the Holy Spirit which would bear fruit at times of tumult, a seed of peace whose fruitfulness would allow me to sow peace into the lives of others when they needed it most, a seed which could only have come from heaven's throne room as the ordination gift of Christ, the Lord of this church and Ruler of the Church, all believers in all places and all times.

I remember the joy when this new congregation in Saskatchewan invited my wife and I to stay on as their pastor. There we were, four years into our first charge, when we came to face another major change: an

Ontario church, Wainsburg, had issued an invitation for us to take up pastoral duties there.

The time for a decision was closing in. Our children would soon hear rumours at school or from other children in Sunday School, so we had to let them know we were thinking of changing churches. Adrian, now eight years old, sat silently absorbing the news. Our youngest, Elayna, just three and a half years old, asked, "Will we move my bed?"

"Of course, Butterfly," I replied. "Your bed and dresser and toys will come with us."

"Okay—ready, we can go!" she declared.

Mom quietly offered that we were waiting for God to give us some clear direction. She went on to explain that usually when we faced such a big decision, we prayed to God—at our family prayers, or in our personal prayers. Somehow He'd answer us and we'd know what our next steps should be.

Around the kitchen table, there was a brief silence as this new information settled into our hearts and brains.

Five-year-old Micah asked, with unrestrained enthusiasm, "Will this new church be closer to Marine Land?"

That past summer, on a visit to Oma and Opa "with the pipe" (the phrase used to distinguish his maternal grandparents from his paternal grandparents, who were called Oma and Opa "without the pipe"), Micah had had the chance to go to Marine Land and enjoy the rides, feed the deer, and stare transfixed by the antics of the killer whales.

Looking into my and his mom's eyes, Micah quickly, smoothingly, added, "I mean, would this new church be closer to Oma and Opa with the pipe?"

His crinkled brows drew together solemnly as if it was the question he'd really meant to ask; he had quickly calculated that Omas and Opas were supposed to be more important than a fun park, even a really fun place like Marine Land.

Oh that Micah, our little thrill seeker, humourist, and happy go-lucky kid.

I nodded. Yes to both—being closer to Oma and Opa with the pipe and closer to Marine Land.

Unable to contain himself any longer, the verbal dam broke for Adrian. His hands clenched in his lap and the short twitches of his nodding head gave sharp emphasis. "You did this to me in Grand Rapids, and now you're doing this again. I lost all my friends when we moved."

Ah, the reason for the tears was explained. Adrian, though young, was always fiercely loyal to his friends. Even now he remembered and missed his little buddies, the children of my seminary classmates who themselves had been scattered from the Philippines to Toronto and many other places. There seemed to be nothing to say. There'd be no way to settle this storm of tears. Tears rolled onto his lasagne, mixing salty tears with little pockets of grease forming tiny sparkling puddles on his food.

The rest of us ate. Lasagne was a favourite and Carolyn didn't always enjoy making it—too many steps. But for this evening, hoping to settle bellies and minds in preparation for our news, she had thought this would be a fitting treat.

There was a deepening silence. The wafting, rich smell of lasagne was made even better by the smell of pie on the counter. The salad on the table had a variety of shades of green, which oddly matched the greens in our checkered tablecloth, the one we'd lose in the move.

Suddenly, a deep voice took us all by surprise: "Richard, *this is God!* Go to Wainsburg!"

How did our five-year-old know my first name? (Usually the people at the church addressed me as "Rev. Vander Vaart" and Micah always called me "Dad.") How'd he manage to get his voice so deep? He'd cupped his hands around his mouth to project, but these deep bass vibrations had never before issued from his lips. Where did he come up with stuff like that?

While driving away from a meeting with one of the youth of our prairie church, I heard a still, quiet thought: "Go to Wainsburg." And what followed was a quiet, reassuring peace.

In the car, at 2:10 in the afternoon while driving the busy main street through town, I remember passing the Christian bookstore. I remember the exact glint of sun across the windshield as I recalled Micah's booming voice: "Richard, *this is God!* Go to Wainsburg!"

Throwing my head back in laughter, all these scenes flitted through my mind, and many, many others, as the movers packed the last things from the house and finally shut the door, latched it, and began pulling away. Our God would take care of us.

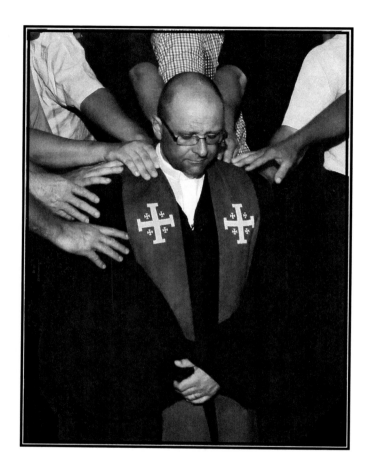

We don't always get to see how our prayers are answered. Or maybe more accurately, it is in hindsight that we understand better how God has answered our prayers.

> *I went on praying and confessing my sin and the sin of my people, pleading with the LORD my God for Jerusalem, his holy mountain. As I was praying, Gabriel, whom I had seen in the earlier vision, came swiftly to me at the time of the evening sacrifice. He explained to me, "Daniel, I have come here to give you insight and understanding. The moment you began praying, a command was given. And now I am here to tell you what it was, for you are very precious to God. Listen carefully so that you can understand the meaning of your vision."* (Daniel 9:20–23)

Note that Daniel, a righteous man, was confessing his sin and the sins of his nation. I know it is often easier for me to explain my sin to God than it is for me to confess it, to openly admit my need for His deep cleansing at the core of who I am.

Note also that the moment Daniel prayed, a command was given. We don't always have a Daniel experience. We rarely see how our prayers move the hand of God and result in the spiritual beings at God's command being dispatched and working out the Lord's will.

Trust that God is moving, acting, and working in ways we won't see until eternity, and once in a great while the living God will send His messengers to explain what we need to understand. It might be an angel. It might be a prayer warrior. It might be circumstances. It might be His gracious no or a wonderful yes. Be assured of this: God is acting.

Note also that we are precious to God. The gift of Christ Jesus makes us precious to God. Our prayers are heard because Christ has come, died, and risen from the dead. Be assured this day that no matter what you are facing, *you* are precious to God.

> O THOU that enlightenest every man that cometh into the world, enlighten our hearts with the brightness of Thy grace, that we may ponder and love those things that are acceptable unto Thee—Amen.
>
> —Priest's Prayer Book, 1870

DECEMBER 3

Beautiful

HE WOULD EASILY BE DESCRIBED AS BEAUTIFUL. HIS HAIR WAS SHORT, VARIOUS tones of deep brown and chestnut, and washed across his scalp in waves that could not have been sculpted. His eyelashes would have been the envy of any runway model, but they suited his face and hazel brown eyes, shielded by very masculine, full eyebrows which kept his features from being feminine. With defined cheekbones, ruddy skin, and mostly straight teeth, his eye teeth seemed to add visual interest to his hesitant smile. He worked out, no question; he walked with such ease and natural steps. So much would draw you to this young man, but he also had a hesitancy that didn't seem to fit.

His girlfriend, Vera, was bringing him to me. Wait, that word—girlfriend—didn't quite work. It is what my mind had filled in rather than what I'd been told.

She spoke first. "Randolph thinks he's gay. He believes he is a Christian. He wants advice."

Talk about blunt; it was machine gun brevity. There was a hardness in her features, not anger. Her straight hair would be described by haughty peers as mousy. Her eyes were nice, but not memorable, and her brows unevenly plucked. It was obvious that of the two of them, he was the beautiful one. She was the natural leader.

Ah, they were friends. He was comfortable with that description. She was hoping for something far different. Little wonder she had brought him to me. Maybe the pastor could offer a book, or a session of counselling, that would change everything.

Randolph shuddered slightly, mostly from nerves and a touch of embarrassment. She reached out her hand, so simply and trustingly, and with familiarity he took it. It was an unconscious gesture on their parts.

Randolph cleared his throat again. He started to describe his proclivities.

I held up my hand. "Wait. Start at the most important part. How do you describe your walk with Jesus?"

Randolph moved his hand away from her and adjusted his chair slightly, away from me. "Jesus just seems too demanding. If I like men, why should that bother Jesus?"

He answered a question with a question, and though it was directed to me, it was Vera who caught the import of the words, admitting his attractions.

Offering the most encouraging smile I could, I gently amended my question: "Who is Jesus in your life? What part does He play?"

"Sunday School stuff mostly," he answered. "Heard that He knocks on the door of my heart and I can let him in, all that sort of thing."

The clear implication: why would Jesus want to step into the troubled cauldron of his emotions and torment?

"Indeed," I said. It was a verbal pause, allowing a second or two before I had to go on with the tough truth: "He stands there. He is prepared to enter into our lives, fully, deeply, honestly, and change our nature. By nature we are sinful. By nature we reject Christ. By nature we hold our wants as the truest direction of our lives. But Christ knows how He made us—He made us for His glory. He made us to delight in Him forever. The deepest longings of our souls are filled only when Jesus is the One who leads us. He offers adventure and fulfilment that I can only outline in simplest terms, because only He knows what you need, what would be best for you, and what would bring healing to the things you don't even realize need to be healed."

Randolph's face hardened at the explanation I'd offered. He then crumbled into a mix of emotions that told me he wasn't comfortable enough to give way to its fullest expression. At that moment I realized that the arrow of God's truth had touched the right target. There was a great need for healing. Something inside him was so wounded, so scarred and scared and oozing, barely even acknowledged in his own conscious thought. So many of the desires of his heart circled around protectively, ignoring the wound.

He stood quickly. The chair wobbled for a moment and firmly crashed down on its four feet.

"Come on, Vera, we're not going to get much out of him," Randolph said.

Bewildered, Vera stood up. She knew the paradox; the very Person who will clear out our hearts is the One who frightens us the most. Holding his hand, she followed him out the door. She looked back at me once, and I wondered if I'd ever see either of them again.

Let the normal patterns of your behaviour, in the light of the Word of God, be shown for what they truly are. Examine your heart and intentions.

> *Its people don't realize that I am watching them. Their sinful deeds are all around them and I see them all… They are all adulterers, always aflame with lust. They are like an oven that is kept hot while the baker is kneading the dough. On royal holidays, the princes get drunk with wine, carousing with those who mock them. Their hearts are like an oven blazing with intrigue.* (Hosea 7:2, 4–6)

What a description. The sinners are like an oven kept hot, prepared for whatever sinful deed or action might attract them. While they are busy with other things, more sins simmer in the background, ready to be cooked up. How very little we know our own hearts. How poorly we understand our need for a Saviour.

Rarely do we acknowledge what is simmering in the background of our lives. What sin is always blazing in the background for you? What is the secret sin for which the oven of your heart is hot? The very same God who watches is the God who sent Christ to retrain our tastes, to drive the sin from our hearts and give us a future. The Father and the Son have poured out the Spirit this Christmas so that we can walk in the joy of the Lord and sin no more.

> BEHOLD, O Father of mercies, I resign myself and all that I have unto Thee. I rely upon Thy bounty for what Thou judgest fit and needful for me. Thy truth and faithfulness is my best security; Thy wisdom is my satisfaction in all events and accidents; Thy power is my support, protection and safeguard. Lead me whither Thou pleasest; and I will follow Thee with a cheerful heart. I refuse nothing which comes from Thy hands, O most loving Father. I submit to Thy orders, and hope that all things shall work together for my good. And I trust in Thy grace, that I shall always do as I do now, steadfastly adhering thus unto Thee, and never suffering anything that befalls me to pull away from this humble faith in Thy wise and Almighty Goodness—Amen.
>
> —Simon Patrick (1626–1707)

DECEMBER 4

Punched

O LORD our God, who hast chased the slumber from our eyes, and once more assembled us to lift up our hands unto Thee, and to praise Thy just judgments, accept our prayers and supplications, and give us faith that maketh not ashamed, confident hope and love unfeigned...
—Prayer from the Greek Church,
composed more than one hundred years ago

IT WAS THE ODDEST BEGINNING TO MY PARTICIPATION IN THE LOCAL MINISTERIAL. A member of my parish, realizing I was new in town and leading my first church after completing seminary studies, figured it would be good for me to participate in the local ministerial association. About forty pastors of various denominations regularly got together for times of prayer, lunch, and encouragement.

The room was full. A few heads bobbed up, acknowledged my presence, and then tucked down and continued in prayer. I was a bit lost.

About the fifth person to bob stopped mid-bob and noted that I was new, saw no one had come to rescue me, and walked over. His hair, naturally rolled into tight curls, would have been the envy of my daughter. He was tall and his steel-framed glasses were a few years out of date. In a few long strides, he crossed the room and swept me up in a bear hug. Too shocked to return it, he released me, and said, "We're kinda huggers here." No kidding.

He placed a chair next to the one he had vacated and invited me to prayer. He then quietly whispered something about how the group members prayed as they felt led to do so, and usually the prayer times lasted an hour, until lunchtime—which, he assured me, was only a few minutes away; I could smell the cooking tomatoes which would obviously be used for some sort of pasta.

What piqued my interest in this band of prayer warriors was their openly expressed care for one another and deep awareness of the lives and ministries of the others around them. Lutherans and Presbyterians, independent church pastors and lay leaders, Pentecostals and a smattering of mainline church leaders, were joined in prayer.

Later their cooperation was affirmed in the hearty meal, eaten together and fully seasoned with laughter and teasing. There were insider jokes and some denominational references in old, corny gags which played out in endless variations. (How many Pentecostals does it take to screw in a lightbulb? Well, a committee was formed, they spoke in tongues, they couldn't take minutes because the interpreter was away that evening, there was hugging and backslapping, and everyone went home feeling better… but the lightbulb never did actually get changed.)

Grabbing lunch was an exercise of poorly directed traffic dashing about trying to get this coffee or that plate, people stepping in front of each other for the sauce; inexplicably it had been placed in a different location than the mixture of pastas (the spaghetti noodles hadn't been sufficient and the kitchen volunteers threw in a bunch of macaroni to fill it out).

Slurping coffee, quiet laughter, and splattering spaghetti accompanied the sounds of genial conversation around the table. Then the chair asked, "So you, the new guy, where are you from?"

Swallowing quickly and clearing my throat of the gluey remnants of spaghetti and macaroni, I said that I was the new pastor at the Christian Reformed Church.

All commotion stopped. Before he could stop himself, the curly-haired hugger Mennonite asked, "Have you been punched yet?"

Confused, I glanced at various other pastors in the room and realized all of them had the same question; he had just been first to voice it.

Near the end of the last pastor's tenure in the church, he'd preached a controversial sermon on marriage. He had strayed slightly from the manuscript and mentioned the word "underwear." One of the strong, near-retirement bricklayers in church had taken great offense to the use of that word, and the topic in general. Getting more and more agitated as the service wended its way to a conclusion, he then followed the minister out of the church, and as the minister stuck out his hand to offer a greeting, the irritated congregant let fly a punch to the gut. The minister doubled over in pain and shock and let out an awful oomph, then went red trying to catch his stolen breath. Without so much as a backwards glance, the congregant squared his shoulders and walked out.

The rest of the church wove in and out, stumbling across one another, unable to sort out what to do next. One of the church ladies led the pastor down the stairs to the coffee area, poured him a cold water, doled out a stale cookie, and left him to wonder what to do next. Buzzing nearby in small knots and clusters, the other church members expressed sharply whispered opinions on what should happen next, but no one actually spoke with the minister. He finally just got up and walked to the parsonage next door.

Sagely nodding, one or two other pastors in the ministerial gathering added a few pertinent details. At least the pastor's wife had been in the nursery and hadn't witnessed the event. His son had bent down and whispered to his gasping dad, "I would have punched him back. I don't think anyone would have blamed you, Dad."

Obviously the story had gained momentum and bizarre variations, none of which could be proven or traced back without great awkwardness.

Blinking hard once or twice, and answering the great silent anticipation around the table, I responded, "No, I haven't been punched yet." A small smile stole across my face as I shrugged, raised my palms skyward, and offered, "But then, I've only been there for six weeks."

RICHARD T. VANDER VAART

Where are you asleep in your faith? Where are you passionate?

Dear children, don't let anyone deceive you about this: When people do what is right, it shows that they are righteous, even as Christ is righteous. But when people keep on sinning, it shows that they belong to the devil, who has been sinning since the beginning. But the Son of God came to destroy the works of the devil. (1 John 3:7–8)

The laity [people in the pews] must repent of wanting a message that makes them comfortable but does not transform them into the image of Christ…

Vance Havner said, "I have observed in the past few years that a strange stupor has fallen over the church of God. They come to church with their fingers crossed, ready to take what they hear with a grain of salt, and the preacher has two strikes against him, before he utters a word. Besides that, the devil has cocained and chloroformed this present age, until a strange coma has settled over the saints… Our eyelids are heavy and our brains are clouded, and unless we stir up the gift of God within us and get down to the business of watching and praying, our Lord shall come suddenly and find us sound asleep."[1]

—Michael Catt

Almighty God, heavenly Father, full of loving-kindness, and our just Judge, when we are confronted about our life—what we think and what we do, the right we don't do and the encouragements we neglect to speak—we must confess that we are not sorely burdened enough with our past sins. Too easily we comment on the sins of others.

Regularly we are bored with the thought of repentance. Confront us. Show us the impact of sins in our lives, the festering in our families, the ruinous attitudes in our communities, the wounding and scarring of our nation, the consequences of how we rebel against Your Kingdom.

Let our desire be stirred by Your Spirit so that we are drawn to the One who is life eternal. Let our desire be rekindled by Your Spirit so

---

[1] Michael Catt, *The Power of Surrender* (Nashville, TN: B&H Publishing Group, 2010), 44–45.

that we will listen more attentively to the voice of the Good Shepherd of our souls. Move us to seek Your forgiveness with all sincerity of heart. Embolden us to offer and receive forgiveness from one another. Wake us. Work in us. Christmas Child, get past our defences and bring us to maturity in our faith. Amen.

DECEMBER 5

Bearded

THE FIRST THING YOU'D NOTICE ABOUT NESTOR WAS HIS GREAT BIG REDDISH beard. It was fascinating to children (in a car accident sort of way), as though they were waiting for something to fall out of it, like maybe a dead bird or bits and pieces of a long past dinner. Then there was the fascination of his hat. It was shaped, sun-bleached leather, and the sweat stains which had dried after each exertion had left a salt residue that looked like tide markers. Nestor was tall and heavy-set. No matter how hot it got in August, he'd always wear a flannel shirt and blue-jean overalls. He moved with a speed that astounded each group of campers who would have their turn to follow him for axemanship training at the boys camp.

While teaching the youth the finer points of using an axe, or differentiating between an axe and a hatchet, he'd tell these campers about the wonders of nature. "Here is a plant that's only found in a few select places on these prairies. Delight in it. Don't disturb it."

The boys were divided evenly into five groups, and over the course of two weeks each group spent at least two sessions with Nestor. Each group received different information on the wildlife in the area. One group got to watch as a snake gorged itself on a huge frog. Another group saw the den of a fox, whose kits were already growing and could be seen across the meadow. Every animal had a place in creation, and all of creation declared the glory of God.

God's creation supplies our needs. Trees fall in the woods and can be used for firewood. Branches can be used to make lean-tos as simple overnight shelters. Nothing need ever go to waste. Nestor would always warn the campers, "*Never* abuse creation. Never harm the creatures God has placed in this beautiful world of ours."

Many a camper would look at this bearded giant and marvel that he could be so tender, such a great steward of the Master's creation, and so massive—and all of this (and more) rolled into one person.

Those who had been especially good in the axemanship course could join Nestor and his cheerful wife Ann and their passel of children for lunch. This was special. They would have lunch at their family home, not a lunch prepared by the volunteer kitchen staff and whichever campers had to be on duty for that particular meal. No, this would be a home-cooked meal, lovingly prepared by a woman who was gifted for it and delighted in preparing great food for her husband. Of course, the campers would speculate as to whether Nester brought home roadkill for the crockpot, since nothing in creation should be wasted. Every single camper wanted the privilege of eating at their home, just to be able to boast, to be able to relate the story of their experiences in hushed voices at the fireside long after the counsellors had gone to bed.

Nestor had a mysterious way of choosing who got to join them for lunch—four kids on the first Thursday and four different kids on the second Thursday. He didn't necessarily choose the best axeman. Perhaps it'd be the one who was kindest to the younger campers. Maybe it'd be the one who listened most attentively.

The day Bob was chosen, he knew he'd have a great story to tell.

Promptly at 11:45 a.m., Bob joined the other three boys on the trek to the house at the top of the hill. While dozens of rowdy, hungry, dusty campers had to form long lines and hope to be among the first to get into the dining hall, Bob and his companions followed the worn path to Nester's home. One of the thoughtful little lads even picked some flowers along the way, carefully avoiding the ones which might be rare, or "endangered" (or whatever it was that Nestor had declared over those petals with such awe).

The long table in Nestor's dining room-kitchen had two long wooden benches that allowed a generous number of visitors, expected or unexpected. The flowers, shyly handed to Ann, were promptly divided into three little bouquets and placed in makeshift vases made of empty baby food jars. The three tablecloths, mismatched, overlapped one another to cover the entire length of the table. After a brief introduction of the four boys, each by name, for Ann's benefit, Nestor waved his huge, hairy hand in the general direction of his various children and said, "These are my children." Ann beamed. The boys waited. But none of the children were named.

Nestor removed his hat, something the campers had never seen. They suppressed giggles. That alone would be worth a good story or two around the campfire. Behind Nestor's back, the campers all had questions. Was he bald? Was he hairy under his hat? Were there critters living there that produced the white substance which ringed the hat?

The unnamed children of Nestor and Ann fell into an awed silence as they waited for their dad to pray. There was, so the four campers later learned, a set prayer to begin the breakfast meal, a prayer which was only ever prayed at lunchtime, and a prayer which was only used for supper. For whatever reason, on this day, in the presence of these campers, Nestor did the unthinkable; he prayed the opening sentence of the evening meal prayer. His children all jerked their heads off their folded hands and stared at their dad. The four campers, alerted by the rustles and shifting, looked up at Nestor's children inquiringly—and then at Nestor himself. Something had gone wrong.

"Oh dammit," he sighed. Then Nestor began again. This time he spoke the words of the lunchtime prayer and the children relaxed their shoulders. Their foreheads each touched their folded hands as the four bewildered campers wondered what had just happened.

How much of our daily walk with God is done by rote, as if the living Lord doesn't see through our divided devotion? The Word today cuts through our inattention.

> *When the LORD first began speaking to Israel through Hosea, he said to him, "Go and marry a prostitute, so that some of her children will be conceived in prostitution. This will illustrate how Israel has acted like a prostitute by turning against the LORD and worshiping other gods."* (Hosea 1:2)

My heart is disgusted by this command given to Hosea, and that is the wrong place to be offended. The really disgusting point is that any sin—my sin—is gross unfaithfulness to God, boredom and inattention in worship, valuing the world above the Word (the Bible and living Word called Jesus), making retirement an idol, and hoarding instead of giving.

All of these, among many other things in our minds, hearts, and actions, are evidences of our prostitution. We forget the grace of God. He spoke to Israel through Hosea. The living God of heaven and earth did not abandon us.

Hosea buys back his wife, just as God the Father gave us Jesus Christ as the bride price while we were still lost in our sin. God is relentless. He is the One who reveals Himself as just, loving, and present until we either turn from our prostitution or turn away from Him forever.

> SPEAK, Lord, for Thy servant heareth. Grant us hears to hear, eyes to see, wills to obey, hearts to love; then declare what Thou wilt, reveal what Thou wilt, command what Thou wilt, demand what Thou wilt—Amen.
> —Christina G. Rossetti (1830–1895)

DECEMBER 6

Mini

NO ONE WAS REALLY SURE HOW SHE GOT HER NICKNAME. A FEW STORIES circulated. Her mother was a Dutch immigrant with a difficult name, Mieke (pronounced Mee-Kah). Mini was born with Down syndrome. Her father checked out immediately; he hadn't signed up for having a little girl who wasn't the perfect child of his imaginings and dreams.

Mieke did her best as a single mom and immigrant in a country that, while similar to her beloved Holland on the surface, was in reality alien. Mieke, according to the mixed and mashed stories, called her daughter "Mini Miek," which was soon shortened to Mini.

As Mini grew, her disabilities became more obvious to her mother than the joyful spirit Mini possessed. In desperation, Mieke brought Mini to the hospital on a Saturday when the doctor's office was closed. A minor ailment was troubling Mini, and having asked an orderly to watch Mini for just a few minutes, Mieke slipped away "to the bathroom." She never came back.

Mini moved from place to place, from one foster home to another, and finally wound up in a group home.

Mini's name stuck, and it would be spoken with a cruel twist by her social worker. Mini, like so many folks with Down syndrome, struggled with her weight. The group home had ample food, easily accessible, and Mini's main worker struggled with weight issues as well. If Mini remained bigger than she was—well, that was okay.

Mini never minded. She didn't speak much, but her smile rippled outwards from her lips, crinkling her nose, brightening her eyes, lifting her brows, and brightening her face. The radiance would sometimes stop strangers.

While Mini was very sensitive to the people around her—caring for those who wept, hugging those who needed one, and hugging many who didn't realize how much they needed one—Mini's worker remained cold, aloof, and just did her job.

One part of the job that the worker hated, absolutely hated—loathed, really—was bringing Mini to church on Sunday mornings and Friendship Group on Wednesday evenings. Friendship Group was hosted by the local church, and many people who were part of the group home came to the church to learn about Jesus, sing songs, have craft time, and of course delight in specially chosen treats. The emphasis here is on *specially chosen*, since many of the clients had peanut allergies. Others had issues with food colouring. A few were allergic to chocolate while loving the taste and smell of chocolate. Then there were the three who had gluten issues, and maybe dairy as well. The tests were inconclusive, but the gastric reactions and foul winds were less inconclusive.

Sighing loudly and folding her arms in order to catch the attention of the other workers, as though telegraphing "I'm here, doing what I'm supposed to, but I don't have to like it," Mini's worker sat down away from her client.

The music began. Mini would sway. She would laugh. She would clap her hands to the beat as long as she could, and when her weight and wheezing slowed her, she would sit, catch the eyes of others around her, and wink or nod or offer her best smile of encouragement. As much as her worker hated being there, Mini soaked up every ounce of pleasure in being in Jesus' house.

What particularly irritated her worker was a gesture Mini made. There were a few songs that included the word *you*: "Jesus Loves You" or "You're My Friend and You Are My Brother." Mini would hold her arms high above her head, uncurl both index fingers, and point them to the worker, singling her out. Sensitive as Mini was, she was absolutely and resolutely oblivious to her worker's reaction.

One Sunday morning, when the pews were especially full, Mini had to be seated right next to her worker. Cold silence emanated from the worker in waves, like an open door allowing winter's blasts to steal warmth and joy from all it encountered. Mini countered with a nod, her biggest reassuring smile, and joy that bubbled up from some mysterious place deep inside her. The worker's reply was folded arms. Ach. Hmph. Squirm. Squirm. Sighhhh.

The music began. For all to see, Mini held her arms way up high and pointed to her worker. In a stabbing whisper, the worker leaned in close to Mini and boiled over: "You are embarrassing me." Slightly louder, voice harder, more like staff to client, she added, "Stop it right now."

Mini's index fingers folded towards her palms, her wrists slackened, and her arms dropped slowly past her head to her lap. She sat still for a moment. Then she leaned over, unconcerned in the least with the worker's stiff posture, rigid arms, and recent reprimand. Mini dropped her head on the worker's shoulder and, as quietly as her thick tongue would allow, whispered, "Jesus not 'barrassed by you. He loves *you*."

This final phrase was all the louder because the final notes of the song had ended and the singers, guitar, drums, and piano had fallen silent. Into that stillness, the piercing words: "He loves *you*" finally pulled together all the hand-waving and finger-pointing, all the radiant smiles of this worker's fat client.

All her persistent winks and nods of encouragement broke past the defending wall of her heart. In the screaming awkwardness of that moment, with rustling papers all around and a few inquiring looks from other staff and church members, Mini was used by the Spirit of the living God to finally, truly, richly communicate the one truth that her worker's heart so achingly needed: Jesus loves *you*.

Who has grabbed your heart with her kindness? Who has shown you great love despite your less than encouraging response?

> *I am writing to remind you, dear friends, that we should love one another. This is not a new commandment, but one we have had from the beginning. Love means doing what God has commanded us, and he has commanded us to love one another, just as you heard from the beginning.*
>
> *I say this because many deceivers have gone out into the world. They deny that Jesus Christ came in a real body. Such a person is a deceiver and an antichrist.* (2 John 5–7)

Yesterday I saw a recipe for marriage. It included four cups of love and one cup of flattery concealed with well-chosen words and even a pinch of kindness for the in-laws. (Yeah, I liked that as well, just a pinch of kindness.)

What I missed was any reference to God. Sure, it might seem marriages can work without God, but the fact of the matter is that all of our relationships are grounded in God's goodness. Whether or not we acknowledge Him, our Father in heaven gives us the gift of relationships: friends, neighbours, coworkers, board members, fellow pewsitters, lovable uncles, and prickly cousins. The fact that God has shown the world His love in Christ is the only ground, the only reason, we can live in love with others. Our own strength fails us.

We are incredibly selfish people. Our own self-serving motives can be hidden from our conscious acting. The call to love is a call for us to look to Christ. The call to love is to first and foremost be devoted to serving our God and King, the outflow of which is living in love, real love that endures wrong, overcomes evil with good, and holds out the confident hope that the victory of God's love will one day be fully shown and fully known.

Loving God and loving those whom He puts in our lives takes a committed decision that will test us to the limit. Love is not easy. Love is not only extended to those who are easy to love.

I remember a wonderful message during which children's letters to God were read. One went something like this: "God, I know we are supposed to love everybody, but you just don't know my brother Bertie." Of course we laughed. But the truth is, the recipe for love begins with, is enriched by, and is completed in Christ.

LIGHTEN our darkness, we beseech Thee, O Lord; and by Thy great mercy defend us from all perils and dangers of this night; for the love of Thy only Son, our Saviour, Jesus Christ—Amen.
—Gelasian Prayer, 492 A.D.

DECEMBER 7

Stubborn

DUTCH IMMIGRANTS FORMED A CHURCH COMMUNITY IN OUR PRAIRIE TOWN fifty years before my wife and I moved there. Immigration had pretty much stopped after the first decade, so it was a pretty big event when a new family came to check the church out and announced they were planning to move into the area. These immigrants from the Netherlands were straight off the boat—actually, off the plane and train—but the accepted label to indicate someone freshly arrived into Canada was "off the boat."

The new family had checked out a variety of churches in the area. One of the churches had the men on benches on the right side of the church while the women and children sat on the left side. That worked for only one week, as this family had seven children and the man's harried, frazzled wife was not signing up to singlehandedly care for all seven with no help from her husband week after week, especially as the service lasted over two hours.

When this man greeted me after service in our church, he introduced himself as Fokke. Given the way he pronounced it, the name had an unfortunate verbal similarity to the well-known F-word frequently abused by teens who seek to be cool with their peers.

I gulped. This would be an interesting challenge.

The majority of people in this church had grown up hearing Dutch names. This one didn't faze anyone, except for the two snickering tweeners who happened to be standing on the steps of the church. Their household heard very little spoken Dutch, as Mom had been born in Canada of an entirely different heritage and Dad's parents had immigrated so long ago that Dutch was spoken only very rarely in his presence.

"Um, can I call you Frank?" I suggested.

"Nee. Fokke is my name," he replied very quickly in the accents which rose so familiarly to my ears and caused the two tweeners to have to step around the corner of the church to give full vent to their laughter. They were now trying to explain to their cousin how this newcomer had just cussed out the minister—and right after church, too.

Fokke then proceeded to ask me if I could help with the immigration process. As they shopped for a farm, found an appropriate school for the kids, looked for reasonably priced second-hand clothes and so on, could we help with translation? Or help them find a retiree in the church who could act in that capacity? I suggested a few people and made introductions at the large coffee urn where the men inevitably gathered to chat and inexplicably block others from easily accessing the coffee.

Well, five days later an exasperated retiree called me to express his frustration. He asked me what could only be described as a trick question: "Do you know how stubborn a Dutchman can be?"

Thankfully, he wasn't really looking for me to answer; it was hysterical to me and rhetorical to him.

"No matter how I trried to steer him in the right direction," the retiree continued, "he wvas determint to buy a farhm on some of the drriest land around here. It is a wvet summer, I told him, and unless he planned to plant cactus, he's going to be in bigk trouble in the next year or two."

His own dialect reflected a particular region of the Netherlands. The more exasperated he got, the more it leaked through. I needed to concentrate in order to fully grasp what he was telling me.

Appropriate announcements were made in church, seeking a work team to help this man's wife clean up the house, which was available for immediate occupancy, amazingly enough. The reason for availability was readily apparent when one of the volunteers and I approached the rabbit warren of structures cobbled together to form a family living space. It was composed of a trailer added to what could only be described as a former barn to which had also been added what might have been a plywood Johnny. Taken together, it was described by the realtor as "a unique, move-in ready, rustic farm-family dwelling." My dignified, very proper volunteer, when she laid eyes on this conglomeration, sighed an appropriate Dutch insult under her breath ("Ratjetoe," which roughly translates to *rat's nest*).

Part of the rustic charm, according to the realtor trying to unload the property after losing a bet, were the hay bales all around the house.

"Look," she said, waving at the house with a sweep of her arm. "It's a wonderful, natural insulation."

City-bred as I am, even I know the hay provided a convenient, multi-access point for all kinds of vermin to nibble, dig, chew, and otherwise find protected, hidden ways into the hodgepodge home.

Sitting on the back bumper of the moving van was the weeping wife. Her frazzled husband was herding their children away from Mom and trying to point out the wonders of their new farmyard and all the interesting things to explore while balancing his second youngest son on his hip. The child added to the cacophony with wails and exclamations of pain over the various scratches and welts he'd gotten from reaching into the raspberry brambles.

Softly, ironically, my cleaning volunteer whispered her opinion about Dad: "You can tell a Dutchman, but you can't tell him much he'll listen to." Given her own thick Dutch accent, it was absurd. The absurdity made me laugh, almost as loudly as the tweeners that fateful Sunday morning.

No matter how many cleaning and scrubbing volunteers descended on that place, it could never be properly cleaned. No matter how many local farmers—who'd spent a couple of decades learning how to coax crops from this particular kind of soil in this dry region—offered their advice, only weeds responded by casting their seeds in proud, reckless abundance. No matter how many rodent traps and mountains of warfarin were placed in the nooks and crevices of the home, the rodents won. All the best advice was lost on this man.

They were going to move away. After their too brief sojourn, we loaded their belongings into a nondescript moving van. The very same son who had scratched his arms and offered screams to greet me on my first visit now munched with delight on his favourite food, raspberry tarts, provided by one of the church's many proficient home bakers.

The man's wife offered her final, impatient words: a summons for her husband to leave the farm and drive. Given her accent and barely concealed anger, it sounded to me and the slack-jawed Canadian-born volunteers who'd helped move their belongings into the van like a twice-repeated obscenity summarizing her true feelings: "F$%@! F@$*!!"

Truly caring for others will stretch us. Showing compassion for the circumstances of others requires denying ourselves and seeing others through the eyes of faith.

> *Then God said to Jonah, "Is it right for you to be angry because the plant died?"*
>
> *"Yes," Jonah retorted, "even angry enough to die!"*
>
> *Then the LORD said, "You feel sorry about the plant, though you did nothing to put it there. It came quickly and died quickly. But Nineveh has more than 120,000 people living in spiritual darkness, not to mention all the animals. Shouldn't I feel sorry for such a great city?"* (Jonah 4:9–11)

Strange, isn't it, what arouses our passions and sorrows? I read in the paper the other day about a man who was dear friends with a woman for eighteen years. He got a parking ticket while visiting her and was fined fifty dollars. He was furious. He believed that because she should have warned him about the new bylaw, she should have paid for half the ticket. Eighteen years of friendship hung in the balance over fifty dollars.

God's passion was not aroused over Jonah's many instances of disobedience. Jonah remained God's prophet. Over and over again, the Lord gave Jonah work to do so that Nineveh would be saved.

Don't be discouraged when you fail. Turn to God. Trust that He will use you for His holy purposes. Especially in this Christmas season, we are reminded that God sent Jesus into the world; God's love reaches beyond Nineveh to the whole world. This Christmas, decide to be obedient, and share the love of Jesus with family and friends.

Bless us today, oh Father, with the realization of Your presence. As we meet in humble paths of service, change for us the tragedy and chaos of a world without You into a prolonged field of honour.

> BLESS us to-day, O Father, with the realization of Thy presence. As we meet in humble paths of service, grant us that consciousness of Thy challenge to each of our lives which shall redeem any labor from seeming trivial, and so change us for the tragedy and chaos of the world without Thee into prolonged field of honor.
>
> Grant us, we pray Thee, to taste in these homeliest activities the joy of being the very knights of God. Give to us now and

always that glorious vision of Thy fellowship which shall strengthen our courage, and transform our halting faith into Christ's certainty of the meaning of life.

Through the same Jesus Christ our Lord—Amen.

—Wilfred T. Grenfell (1865–1940)

DECEMBER 8

Afraid

ONE OF THE GREAT FEARS OF THOSE WHO ARE TRAINING FOR THE MINISTRY is public prayer. We are expected to gather up the requests of our congregants through the course of the week and craft a prayer that honours God and brings the real life of real people before the One who alone hears and answers prayer. It is daunting.

At times of funerals, our prayers are supposed to express our confident faith and offer reassurance to the family of the deceased and include all the names of important family members, all the while keeping their names straight. Given the tangle of divorces and remarriages and those who keep their maiden names and those who shed them, it can be confusing. Weddings can be tough as well, as it happens more and more often that the bride and groom, though faithful Christians themselves, have a huge assortment of old roommates and friends who are not church-goers at all; prayers are a wholly unfamiliar ritual to them, which results in attendants tugging on various and sundry articles of clothing or body parts while much of the congregation has their heads bowed and eyes closed. Of course, the wedding is taped, so every time the happy couple plays their wedding DVD they'll have a chance to witness what no one should have to see.

A great fear for some seminarians is the prayer request. Sometime before a pastoral prayer, the student minister is asked to hear the people as they gather in the church to offer their requests. The student must then remember their names, remember their requests, and formulate a prayer that is honourable and accurate.

The first stumble I ever experienced in this regard made me so very cautious. It was a holiday weekend, so the turnout for church was not too large, which in turn made those who were present more comfortable to speak their requests. It was a long list, longer than the paper which I had taken with me, and I was making small notes and scribbles trying to fit everything onto the little paper.

Well, the prayer opened smoothly with adoration of God. Then there was a brief time of confession, which included one or two of the requests. Next came thanksgiving. You see, the prayer was following an outline of ACTSs: adoration, confession, thanksgiving, supplication (or requests), and submission.

At the point of praying for our collected supplications, the gathered people broke into ripples of laughter. I'd been earnestly praying for the sister of a woman named Sally. This woman had a pretty serious diagnosis, and she required a biopsy to confirm this diagnosis. Unfortunately, in my flustered state I confused the word biopsy with autopsy. To make matters worse, I'd prayed that the sister's autopsy would go well and she'd make a full recovery.

It was several more months before I was ready to tackle prayer requests with any level of ease. When the summer arrived, and I saw that the faithful had been reduced from masses of people to just a few dozen, I thought it time to strike out once again and hear requests before prayer time.

Immediately Sally shot up her hand; the fiasco of a few months before had not deterred her, and her dear sister was in need of prayer. Sally asked that we pray for Samantha, who would be undergoing a mastectomy. This was but the first request and several other requests were shouted out, one after another, so that I had trouble fully filling out the requests. I had to rely on short scratches of information and my memory. That was my first mistake.

This time, as I prayed, there was some embarrassed coughing and twitters of laughter. Now what? Sally's sister Samantha had dropped from first place to somewhere in the middle of the requests and I felt strapped to correctly remember all the information. So, in praying for Samantha, I prayed for her vasectomy, instead of mastectomy, and I didn't catch it.

At the door, after the service, Sally was one of the first people out the door. In a loud voice, she corrected the embarrassing mix-up. She spoke in her high nasal voice. "Pastor, as we have an evening service, would you please pray for Sam? And this time remember that it is a mastectomy." I slightly reddened in embarrassment near the end of the service as I realized my mistake, and now I could feel my ears get red as well.

"Of course," I stammered as graciously as I could. "I'll remember Samantha this evening in the church prayers and correct this."

Sally gave a quick bob of her head and sashayed out the door of the church.

For some reason, it felt to me as if pressure was building on me all day to get this right. Though I'd been here for a few months and had learned to get past my mistakes, there would always be at least one in a worship service. Somehow this mistake and this correction seemed to be a bigger deal, as it was the second time I'd messed up on prayers for Sally's sister.

Thankfully, there were very few requests in the evening service. You could tell the people were listening with more attention than usual. I launched into the prayer. After my prayers for Samantha, there was an audible huff from the general vicinity of Sally and sprinkles of suppressed, awkward laughter.

Now what? I thought as I continued the prayer.

Dark as a storm cloud, Sally marched right up to me after the evening service and blurted out, "As I've already told you, she is not scheduled for a hysterectomy, it is a mastectomy." Then, in as proper and controlled a voice as she could muster, she added primly, "Reverend, be so kind as to refrain from praying for my sister, or she won't have anything left to take out!"

What a great gift the living God gives us through prayer: true communication between the Almighty and His people.

Which of you fathers, if your son asks for a fish, will give him a snake instead? Or if he asks for an egg, will give him a scorpion? If you then, though you are evil, know how to give good gifts to your children, how much more will your Father in heaven give the Holy Spirit to those who ask him!" (Luke 11:11–13, NIV)

A tragedy strikes you or someone close to you, and you are hurting. So you go to God in prayer, and you ask him to comfort you. Do you realize what God does? He doesn't give you comfort. Instead he gives you the Holy Spirit, who is called the Comforter. The Holy Spirit literally comes to dwell in you and put the very comfort of Christ inside of you as you walk through your pain.[2]

—David Platt

The Holy Spirit gives us words to speak that are meaningful. The Holy Spirit shows us the gift of friends who are present and silent. The Holy Spirit builds and affirms community when we are broken. The Holy Spirit living within us directs all our living as we allow Him.

O GOD, who purifiest the heart of man from sin, and makest it more white than snow, pour down upon us the abundance of Thy mercy; renew, we beseech Thee, Thy Holy Spirit within us, that we may show forth Thy praise, and, strengthened by Thy grace, may obtain rest in the eternal mansions of the heavenly Jerusalem; through our Lord Jesus Christ—Amen.

—Sarum Breviary, 1085 A.D.

---

[2] David Platt, *Radical: Taking Back Your Faith from the American Dream* (Colorado Springs: CO, 2010), 57.

DECEMBER 9
Awkward Church Hospitality

BETJE (PRONOUNCED "BETCHA") WAS A JOYFUL LADY, SHORTER THAN AVERAGE height, with a very full head of hair stylishly coifed. Her clothes always reflected a unique offbeat flair. Her English was inflected with a full seasoning of Dutch accents. Once in a while, to the discerning ear, there'd be a great hint of the region from whence her parents had emigrated, and she had unmistakeable pride in belonging to that particular subset of Dutch people.

However, Betje also had a knack for saying exactly the wrong thing with the best intentions. After a young man had just made profession of faith, she purposefully strode over to him, broke into the group of young people surrounding him, and stated, "It is a gud thing you haf done. God be wvid you. Now you vill reelly suffer." The group of boys and girls froze, waited until she was almost out of earshot, and began giggling and tittering and wondering what that could possible mean.

Another time, at the Thanksgiving Day service, a time when many people make extra special efforts to clothe themselves in their best outfits, Betje saw a woman standing at the door. This visitor was hovering near the entryway, unsure where the rest of her family was, when the language-impaired friend swooped down to compliment this newcomer's dress: "What a vonderful dress. I remember how in the war in Holland, when we had no money, I had a dress just like dat one."

Betje beamed and nodded and blinked several times awaiting the stranger's response to the intended compliment, and looked a bit put off to see this other woman's mouth come to a firm line, her eyes hardening slightly as she marched away towards the bathroom.

As a pastor, I often felt the sting of her words, fired at me BB-gun-style. It might be a day or a month later that the true intention of her words would be discerned or explained, or the welt on my ego would disappear all on its own. It took me a number of months to really understand something about this woman, her love of God, and her desire to truly be a blessing.

One incident made things a lot clearer for me.

There are some sermons which flow from the fingertips, across the keyboard, and onto the screen with ease. The Bible text falls open like a ripe peach and the juices and flavour of the intended message are sweet for all to receive. Others... well, others are like figs. Figs are an acquired tasted. They can be tasty, but finding the formula and right recipe requires a lot more patience and work. Trial and error is involved.

I had such a text before me that week. For some reason, rather than working with easier material, I struggled through a couple of different half-baked ideas and discarded many. Finally, as Sunday dawned, I realized I had to go with what I had. The morning service was filled with people. That service and sermon were fine. However, in our tradition we had two services per Sunday. The evening service was not usually as well attended, but those who come were quite engaged and could be critical. Sometimes they were seeking deeper understanding, other times to display their own knowledge, and still other times to just be ornery and push back.

The afternoon slowly creaked by, as I couldn't quite leave the evening sermon alone. I tinkered. I fussed. I agonized over the placement of a semicolon. Finally, pleased with the overall interpretation of the text but a bit hesitant about the way in which it might be presented to the congregation for their ingestion, I stepped into the pulpit. The service started well. The people sang full-out the well-loved hymns and recited the psalm-reading which fitted that Sunday. The sermon began after an appropriate invocation to God, asking His Spirit's guidance, and the squirming began with the opening sentence.

Unable to avert my eyes, I saw Betje rubbing her shoulders against the back of the pew. There'd be a small scowl and I knew I'd be hearing about this sermon later. She moved her shoulders up and down and pressed back against the bench as if recoiling in horror. A note of irritation crept into my voice, not too discernible by the congregation, but enough to have my wife raise her eyebrow at me as if to inquire, "What is *wrong* with you?"

As I preached, I managed to present the sermon and narrative. In the back of my mind, though, I stewed over the incredible rudeness of this woman. She was seated close enough that I could see every exaggerated sigh. I noted every shift across the bench and every sag of Betje shoulders. I'd wait a day or two and then I'd tell her how rude she'd been. Yes, that was my decision as the sermon drew to a conclusion.

Unlike many of my colleagues, I don't take Mondays off. I find them to be a good, quiet day to be in the office and get a start on organizing the week. Around 11:00 a.m., this woman—red-faced, hurried, and for once a bit dishevelled—and her quiet, godly husband arrived unannounced at my office. It was hard to conceal the scowl as I remembered the previous evening's antics.

Popping her head in through the doorway, Betje noted, "Pastor, I vanted you to know dat I vas very uncomfortable in church last night."

In response, all I could do was grimace. The words I wanted to serve up at that particular moment weren't either appropriate or savoury.

Without noticing all the turmoil brewing within me, Betje continued. "I just got back from the doktor, and I haf shingles. I vas already so sore last night, itchy, but I didn't vant to miss your preaching. Please pray for dis shingles be done quick."

And with these words, she and her husband left the office in order to fulfill the prescription and get home and try to find some relief. And "dis pastor" realized that things are not always as they appear; I had a long way to go to learn to govern my thoughts and opinions.

CAN'T HELP MYSELF

When do you return to your misconceptions of a person or situation, rather than truly seek to find out what's going on? Only when we truly know through investigation and questions can we address a problem or make something right.

And when people escape from the wickedness of the world by knowing our Lord and Savior Jesus Christ and then get tangled up and enslaved by sin again, they are worse off than before. It would be better if they had never known the way to righteousness than to know it and then reject the command they were given to live a holy life. They prove the truth of this proverb: "A dog returns to its vomit." And another says, "A washed pig returns to the mud." (2 Peter 2:20–22)

God of our life, there are days when the burdens we carry chafe our shoulders and weigh us down; when the road seems dreary and endless, the skies grey and threatening; when our lives have no music in them, and our hearts are lonely, and our souls have lost their courage. Flood the path with light, run our eyes to where the skies are full of promise; tune our hearts to brave music; give us the sense of comradeship with heroes and saints of every age; and so quicken our spirits that we may be able to encourage the souls of all who journey with us on the road of life, to Your honour and glory—Amen.
—St. Augustine (354–430)

DECEMBER 10

Wigs

VISITING AKKER WAS ALWAYS AN ADVENTURE. SHE WAS A DIGNIFIED WOMAN who was always very nicely dressed. Whenever I visited, no matter the day, she'd be wearing something appropriately stylish; for example, one of her favourites was an ashes-of-rose dress with a soft cream-coloured ruffle at the front and the ever-present three-strand faux pearl necklace, slightly oversized. Sometimes she'd be in a wheelchair, other times she'd be lying on her bed, but during the day she always dressed herself with careful attention. Unlike so many others who filled the rooms and halls of the nursing home, she would never, ever be found wearing a tracksuit.

The nursing home had long hallways which during the day were filled with residents in wheelchairs, lined up to go to various baths, activities, dayrooms, or perhaps just be positioned someplace visible so they'd have the chance to interact with whomever might be visiting that day.

After negotiating the hallway and rounding the last corner to her room, I'd have to pause and say rather loudly, "I sure hope Akker is in today, the dominee is visiting." Akker, like so many in that prairie congregation, was an immigrant from the Netherlands, and the word she used for minister was still the Dutch word, *dominee*. If there was no response, I'd have to knock and say a bit louder, "I wonder if Akker is in today?"

Sometimes I'd hear some shuffling and an urgent, "No, no, not yet, dominee." Other times I'd hear a thickly accented voice saying, "Ya, come in."

As a new pastor to the area, I hadn't yet learned all the rituals, nor had I yet acquired the necessary patience that comes with experience. On one early visit, I came into the room too quickly. There she was, rummaging desperately through her underwear drawer, the one she could most easily reach, searching for her wig. I saw the few strands of hair she had left wildly wafting about her ears and eyebrows as she moved her head and continued her search. Later I learned that if I delayed a bit, but not quite long enough, her wig might be askew, placed sideways and oriented ear to ear instead of forehead to back. She'd wear her wig, no matter its orientation, like the snow-crowned glory of old age promised in Proverbs.

Once in a while, all I'd see is Akker sitting regally in her wheelchair, her hands having smoothed down the errant wisps of hair, arms calmly laid on the rests of her chair, a few unmentionables (bras and panties) caught in the half-closed drawer and madam herself trying as inconspicuously as possible to catch her breath.

Doris, a very loud, hale, and well-met resident in the same nursing home, would wheel herself from room to room. For some reason, Doris had taken a shine to Akker's wig. If the short-haired nicely styled grey-white wig was in reach and Akker was not paying attention, Doris would steal it. Without shame, and quicker than you'd expect of an oversized woman poured into a slightly too small wheelchair, Doris would enter Akker's room and seize the wig from the pillow, or plunge her hand into the underwear drawer on a fishing expedition.

Regardless of the state of her pate, Akker would welcome her dominee. She never remembered my name, she couldn't quite recall the name of our church, and she lamented the fact that her sons and daughters had long ago left the church. But this one thing she remembered: "I will see the goodness of the Lord in the land of the living." Sometimes she'd speak a line of Psalm 27 in Dutch, the very words she'd memorized many distant decades ago as a young girl attending a Christian day school in a rural province. Sometimes she sang a phrase or two of the psalm under her breath, "The Lord is my light and my salvation, whom shall I fear…"

Later I learned to check the hallway just past Akker's room. You see, if it was past the morning coffee and cake break time, Doris would have already had her chance to snatch Akker's wig. I'd look down the next corridor, and if Doris was sitting there with her own poker-straight chestnut hairpiece and the stolen grey-white wig balancing on top, I'd know she'd already been successful in her morning hunt. The second wig would sit like a bird's nest on top of the chestnut hair. It was head-shakingly strange to see a large woman with age spots, whitened eyebrows, browning teeth, and age-lined face wearing a bright chestnut wig with a second wig jauntily crowned upon it.

It was odd to me that the staff never worried about Doris' wig-stealing ways, unless they knew Akker's minister would be visiting. Then Doris would be relieved of her trophy and Akker prepared for the visit. You really never did know what to expect as you walked down those halls.

But this much I learned from my visits with Akker. Planted somewhere deep in her heart, and infrequently recalled from the foggy recesses of her Alzheimer's-shrouded neural pathways, was a soul that would reveal itself as clinging to a joyful hope: "I will see the goodness of the Lord in the land of the living."

To my eyes, no goodness could be unearthed in that dreary place. To my olfactory senses, assaulted by bleach vapours in the hallways, laundry soap near the games room, and unsettling fumes by the kitchen, nothing appetizing remained there. Yet what my eyes hadn't yet learned to see, nor my other senses learned to discern, was the faith that sickness, circumstances, abandonment, dementia, and old age could not dim.

True vision is to see people as image-bearers, people who have the stamp of the divine. This is the law of God.

> *When people do not accept divine guidance, they run wild. But whoever obeys the law is joyful. Words alone will not discipline a servant; the words may be understood, but they are not heeded.*
> (Proverbs 29:18–19)

A few days ago, our foster son asked me, "Richard, where are you going this evening?"

I said I was joining some friends for some street evangelism.

"You're a pastor," he said. "That's not right!"

Wondering what had provoked such a reaction, I realized he might not know the word *evangelism*. "What do you think evangelism means?"

"It's when you go out with a spray can and paint walls with graffiti."

"Oh buddy," I said, "that's vandalism. Evangelism is when you tell people about Jesus."

He nodded. "Oh, that sounds more like you."

How easily we misunderstand words or fill in our own definitions. The Word of God is divine guidance, and as such requires study, rereading, and then implementation. Read. Meditate. Study the Word of God and put it into practice.

> O GOD, who tellest the number of the stars, and callest them all by their names; heal, we beseech Thee, the contrite in heart, and gather together the outcasts, and enrich us with the fulness of Thy wisdom; through Christ our Lord—Amen.
> —Sarum Breviary, 1085

DECEMBER 11

Obedience

SUNDAYS AFTER CHURCH WAS SACRED TIME FOR MY WIFE AND MYSELF. AFTER A busy couple of days leading up to the morning worship service, we were often ready to have the house to ourselves, to have the telephone fall silent, and if we could time things just right, have the children in bed for naps and quiet times. What bliss it was.

Our church made this quite a challenge.

First there would be the inevitable coffee chat at church. Various members of the church, who had all week to call and register their complaints and concerns or indicate their desire for a visit, would remember their message each time I tried to raise my coffee mug to my lips, and I'd have to write down this or that. It wasn't unusual for me to leave the coffee time with a list of fifteen or more things to remember as I once again was forced to pour a mug of cold coffee down the drain in the church kitchen.

The second challenge to pop up would often be an elder who had wanted to go to seminary, who'd studied a few things on his own, and now, as the church had nearly emptied of people, decided to challenge me on some fine point of a text or illustration.

"Can we meet later?" I'd plead. "Say, tomorrow or Tuesday?"

"What if I forget?" he'd shoot back.

Under my breath, I'd long to say, "We'd both be better off for that!" But instead I'd say, "Tuesday it is. 10:00 a.m. at the Pancakes and Bacon Coffee Joint." Perfect.

If all went well, there would be no third challenge. But usually all did not go well. I'd arrive at home to find my wife shouting into the parsonage: "Anyone who does not have the last name Vander Vaart had better be out of this house by the time I count to ten."

On a good day, only a fridge door would slam and a Lego tower would get knocked over as the gaggle of children rushed out by the count of six. On a bad day, my dear, blonde-haired, fair-skinned bride would redden furiously as she sought to outshout the hissing and meowing of our cat, who might be swinging by the tail or scratching to get out of a trap designed by one of the children roaming freely through our house in his boots.

Another child, tired of waiting for the bathroom, would be peeing against the little bush by the backdoor.

"What?" he'd whine as he continued peeing. "When we're at home and the bathroom is busy, we pee outside."

Great.

On the worst days, the challenge might involve my wife being caught mid-yell by a parent of one of these little house-wrecking ruffians.

"Are you yelling at my child?" the parent would darkly ask.

Calmly, my wife would respond, "Are you going to replace the cream which your little angel is drinking straight out of the cardboard container?"

No matter how often we laid the ground rules, the Sunday ritual at the doorway of the parsonage would always be the same: "Anyone who does not have the last name Vander Vaart had better be out of this house by the time I count to ten."

And our three kids would cry, whine, and shout in reply, "Now who are we supposed to play with?"

Obedience is such a challenge. Parents want their children to obey them. The awkward part is that parents live with their children, who see their parents at their best and at their worst. Living for Jesus requires us to live for Him in our relationship with Him and in the ways we relate to others.

> *Lord, you are mine! I promise to obey your words! With all my heart I want your blessings. Be merciful as you promised. I pondered the direction of my life, and I turned to follow your laws.* (Psalm 119:57–59)

Tomorrow. Yeah, I'll start my weight loss tomorrow. I'll, um, start my regular devotion routine tomorrow, or for sure by Wednesday, probably.

Starting. That can be so hard. The psalmist is ready to grab the blessings God pours out, and he deeply desires God's mercies. He needed to turn from the present course to chart a new course of obeying God.

Obedience is not hard. Understand that obedience to God means moving to the place where God pours out His blessings in our lives. As one instructor used to speak in blessing, "Let us meet at the spout where the blessings of God pour out." What a great picture: showers of blessings for those who walk in obedience.

No more excuses. Start today and be prepared for His mercy and abundant blessings.

> LOOK upon us and hear us, O Lord our God; and assist those endeavors to please Thee which Thou Thyself hast granted to us; as Thou hast given the first act of will, so give the completion of the work; grant that we may be able to finish what Thou hast granted us to wish to begin.
> —Mozarabic Prayer, before 700 A.D.

DECEMBER 12

Sleep

IT WAS AN OFF-HANDED COMMENT, HALF-JEALOUS AND HALF-RESENTFUL, THAT our daughter-in-law Jess jokingly made about her husband, Adrian. "Seriously, I think he falls asleep even before his head hits the pillow!"

Jess and my wife Carolyn had shared their difficulties falling asleep and staying asleep. Carolyn has struggled all her life with sleep issues and it was strange to hear that this was true for Jessica as well. It brought to mind something of God's goodness in Adrian's life.

After our long trip from Grand Rapids to our congregation in Saskatchewan, it was obvious that Adrian's little brain was overtaxed with images of our travels, with his loss of little friends and playmates, and with all the newness of the house and neighbourhood. During the day he was a pretty happy child, but at night, wow, the nights were tough.

Adrian shared a room with his brother, Micah. Carolyn was nervous about this, as their room was all the way down the hall from us, past Elayna's room, through the kitchen to the back landing and then down the stairs. Then past the bathroom and near the loud furnace, and there, at the end of the basement hallway, in the farthest corner away from us, was their room. It was a dream for the newly minted "big boys," and in the morning they could slip out of their beds and go into the huge family room and play with their Legos and Mom and Dad would never be the wiser. As Elayna got older, she was a tiny bit jealous of their freedom, but not so enamoured of their great distance from Mom and Dad's room.

It all began about two weeks after we'd settled in the parsonage. All the toys were unpacked, the beds set up, the pictures hung, and the boxes for storage properly put away. Many people from the church were dropping by or inviting us to visit.

The days were a blur. But the nights... well, the nights were a challenge.

Carolyn and I would drop into bed exhausted, and around 2:00 a.m. the screams began. It sounded like one of the boys was being stabbed. From a dead sleep to keen alertness, Carolyn and I jumped out of our waterbed, as best as the waves would allow, and rushed downstairs to the boys' room. Micah was moaning in his sleep at the disturbance, but Adrian was sitting up in his bed, his little arms propped behind him and his blonde hair mussed up. The whites of his eyes were eerily large and his mouth opened so wide that in the dim light spilling in from the hallway we could see his tongue curling around the scream.

Sometimes this would last a few minutes and he'd promptly fall back to sleep. We'd stumble back to our rooms through the maze of books, crayons, and papers on the floor. Other times the screams would be punctuated by gasps for breath, his eyes riveted to a terror unseen to us but all too real to him. He would shake and gather more breath and scream. In the morning, especially after these longer episodes, he'd walk around with big dark rings under his eyes... as would his parents.

The doctor explained that it was night terrors, and nothing to be concerned about. When his brain had processed all the intricacies of the move, all the newness and the grief, he would settle down and sleep better. "Don't wake him," the doctor said. "Just know he will settle down, eventually."

So for weeks we battled all the assaults of our young son's overactive imagination.

In the morning he'd look at me, tearful, and say, "Dad, we prayed. Why didn't Jesus answer?"

What a great question. What a horrible feeling to be his dad, his protector, his mentor in the gift of prayer, and see no answer but another night of screams.

At night, after our customary story reading, he'd ask me, urgently, "Pray with me, Dad." Each night, with increasing fervour, I joined hands with him and asked anew for God's grace to wash away the terrors of the night and give dreams fresh and bright.

It began to seem that these night terrors were taking on a power that was beyond us. Would we never be free of them?

The first night of real sleep hit us like a thunderclap. Carolyn and I both sat up in bed at the same time, intending to look one another in the eye and ask, "What happened? Did you get up and I not hear it? Or is it possible maybe you got up and I didn't feel it?" The sudden movement of all that water in the bladder of the bed caused such upheaval that we first had to land beside the bed and hold tight to the bumper pads.

"Did you get him last night?" I asked, leaning forward.

"No. Did you?"

"No."

We both hurried downstairs to see the boys, sleeping in, looking peaceful and rested, the demon of night terrors remembered no more. What a great gift it was.

Obviously this gift still attends Adrian, as sleep comes to him so easily now, as Jessica has given testimony. It is easy to forget all the victories we've been given, especially as others may still be struggling in those very places where we now stand in victory.

I still remember that evening more than eighteen years ago when Adrian looked at me with huge eyes, widened by expanding realization, and asked, "Do you think, maybe, Jesus heard my prayer? Do you think He gave me sleep?"

Giving thanks for answered prayer is often neglected in our faith walk. Sometimes we even forget what we asked for in our torrent of requests. Whenever we remember or recognize answered prayer, it is wise to honour the Triune God with our praise and thanks.

> *Give thanks to the L*ORD*, for he is good!*
> *His faithful love endures forever.*
> *Give thanks to the God of gods.*
> *His faithful love endures forever.*
> *Give thanks to the Lord of lords.*
> *His faithful love endures forever.*
> *Give thanks to him who alone does mighty miracles.*
> *His faithful love endures forever.*
> *Give thanks to him who made the heavens so skillfully.*
> *His faithful love endures forever.* (Psalm 136:1–5)

> *Say this to those who worship other gods: "Your so-called gods, who did not make the heavens and earth, will vanish from the earth and from under the heavens."* (Jeremiah 10:11)

> [It strikes me that] this is exactly what has happened; all of the 'gods' of that time have indeed literally vanished. We dig them up from the earth. At the time those words were written, this would have seemed the least likely thing imaginable.[3]
> —Dr. Murray Adamthwaite

ALMIGHTY and merciful God, who art the Strength of the weak, the Refreshment of the weary, the Comfort of the sad, the Help of the tempted, the Life of the dying, the God of patience and of all consolation; Thou knowest full well the inner weakness of our nature, how we tremble and quiver before pain, and cannot bear the cross without Thy Divine help and support. Help me, then, O eternal and pitying God, help me to possess my soul in patience, to maintain unshaken hope in Thee, to keep that childlike trust which feels a Father's heart hidden beneath the cross; so shall I be strengthened with power according to Thy glorious might, in all patience and long-

---

[3] Dr. Murray Adamthwaite, "Unravelling Myths About Myths," *Creation*. Volume 37, Issue 1, January 2015, 44–46. Adamthwaite is an archaeologist with a BA in Philosophy, History, and Philosophy of Science, as well as a Ph.D in Ancient History, Languages, and Literature.

suffering; I shall be enabled to endure pain and temptation, and, in the very depth of my suffering, to praise Thee with a joyful heart—Amen.
—Johann Habermann (1516–1590)

DECEMBER 13

GEMS

GEMS. THAT STANDS FOR "GIRLS EVERYWHERE MEETING THE SAVIOUR." OUR church had such a group, a place where young girls from Grades Three to Eight could come and enjoy a time of meeting with other girls, be mentored by Christian teenaged girls and women, do a craft, have a Bible study, and enjoy times of praise. There is something wonderful about young girls who give their hearts in praise. One of our leaders was very gifted in putting together actions for the songs so that the girls and women could sing with their voices, with their hands, and with their hands and feet all in motion bringing praise and honour to God.

Every now and again there'd be a reason for me to be in church on the nights the GEMS met. Sometimes I'd find a reason to be there—maybe I suddenly had an urgent need to photocopy or file something. Any excuse would do to see these youth delight in the presence of God. It was holy.

The GEMS had been meeting since September, and now it was time for their GEMS Sunday. What that meant is parents and guardians, grandparents and siblings, were invited to come to a worship service and hear the songs and learn the Bible themes which these girls were learning. It was always a fun service.

However, this year, the lead counsellor of the GEMS approached me a few weeks before the service. She was concerned. For the first time, not only would the GEMS be singing in church, but two of the girls would read scripture in response to the songs, or they would read the passages on which the songs were based, and four of the girls would lead in the hand-waving, foot-stomping, body-moving praise to the Lord.

Her hesitation made sense to me. You see, some twenty years ago, the denomination was embroiled in the question of whether or not women could be leaders in the church. Having a young girl read the Bible might be offensive to a few of the staunch members of the church. It would be an even bigger stretch to have these youngsters swinging and singing.

"What should I do, pastor?" the counsellor asked me.

Great question. Oddly enough, as a congregation we had long prayed that this faith, the faith of our fathers and mothers, would be communicated through the generations, that our children and grandchildren would claim it as their own. Seeing them up front would be an answer to their prayers, right?

The counsellor drew the corners of her lips together into a tight pucker, as if she'd just tasted bile, then relaxed a bit. "Are you sure? I mean, really sure?"

"What could go wrong?" I confidently returned. "Besides, if there are any concerns, I'll let people know they can talk with me."

For a moment, I thought the counsellor was going to pat me on the head, condescending to me as if I were an overzealous child, asking to accomplish something way beyond my years.

Then she smiled and shrugged. "Okay."

And off she went, whistling the GEMS theme tune, "Jesus Is All the World to Me," which was quickly becoming for me a wonderful brain worm.

The GEMS Sunday quickly approached. It just so happened that the Santa Claus Parade fell on the prior Saturday, and the parade was a cause of scorn for many members of my conservative parish. They considered it odd to encourage a child to believe in Santa and then a few years later rip this belief from them. So it was a surprise to me, big enough to have been measured on the Richter scale, to see a couple of the old sour set standing at the curb with a brood of their grandchildren. I could see them clearly from my vantage point, a few people back, but their focus was on the floats and ponies and shrieks of delight uttered by their grandchildren.

Even now it is a funny, jarring, poignant memory. The clowns were throwing candy canes and other assorted wrapped Christmas candy treats and these children were elbowing people and pulling others away in order to get a bigger share. The grandparents were pointing, laughing, stamping their feet. It was a sight beyond description as their demeanour in church, in public, and in their homes was always so utterly reserved. I figured I was seeing the furthest extent of their antics.

I was wrong. When Santa's float rounded the street corner and came into full view, I watched these four grandparents wave their hands to get the attention of their miscreant grandkids and then call out, louder and louder until the crowd took up their cheer, "Santa's here. *Santa's here! Santa's here!*"

Transfixed, I openly stared. My mind sang out, *Who'd have thunk it, these seniors crying out with such abandon, humouring their grandkids? Tomorrow will be such a breeze as some of their grandchildren, and the children and grandchildren of other church members and community folks, get involved in a celebrative service.*

It wasn't a breeze. It was more of a contained hurricane.

The GEMS entered the church in procession. A few flags and a banner went before them. Parents giggled. Girls discretely waved. Others straightened their uniforms and scarfs, the correct uniform of a GEM. The opening parts of the worship service flowed simply, intentionally seeking to make people who were new to church more comfortable.

After the second hymn, the GEMS and their leaders were called forward. They were wonderful. I sat in the front row, having just left the stage in order to make room for these girls and their leaders and take the focus off myself. I couldn't see what was going on behind me. All I could feel was the joyful abandon of praise the girls offered. It took me a while to notice the increasing awkwardness of the adult leaders with them.

The hairs on my neck began to prickle. Something was wrong. As casually as I could, I looked back and saw these same four grandparents who'd I'd seen the day before at the parade, now with exaggerated frowns, arms folded, and eyes glaring. Ah, the winds were picking up.

As soon as the service was done, I thanked the GEMS and their leaders profusely. It was my intention to let all present see the support of the church leadership for their delightful praise to God and the wonderful way in which they were communicating all the Bible truths they'd learned so far.

As the GEMS processed out, I followed quickly behind and managed to stand by the doors where I knew the fearsome foursome would exit. When they did, I jerked my head towards the small space away from those who were leaving church, the little landing near the stairs to the unused balcony.

There, the four began to vent.

"Disgusting," one spat out. "Aerobics in church!"

Another raised her voice. "Who makes such a display in public?"

In the loudest whisper I thought I could get away with, so as not to affect the smiling people leaving the sanctuary, I hissed, "Santa's here!"

Confused, they looked at one another, blinking in exaggeration and shaking their heads.

Suddenly one of them realized I had seen them at the parade. That I'd seen their public displays and shouting, their own public aerobics for a cause far less worthy.

One by one, humbled, they passed by me and went downstairs. Instead of venting their venomous opinions to their children and grandchildren, they offered quiet words of affirmation.

In the grand scheme of things, perhaps it was a tiny victory; in that little prairie church, it was a ground-shaking change.

Styles of worship is always a minefield for churches. What follows is one of the great pictures we have in the Bible of the splendour of the throne room and voluptuous praise which ever fills those sacred halls.

> *Day after day and night after night they keep on saying, after night they keep on saying, "Holy, holy, holy is the Lord God, the Almighty—the one who always was, who is, and who is still to come."*
>
> *Whenever the living beings give glory and honor and thanks to the one sitting on the throne (the one who lives forever and ever), the twenty-four elders fall down and worship the one sitting on the throne (the one who lives forever and ever). And they lay their crowns before the throne and say, "You are worthy, O Lord our God, to receive glory and honor and power. For you created all things, and they exist because you created what you pleased."* (Revelation 4:8–11)

When a hockey player manages a hat trick in a game where two rival teams are battling it out, the fans shout and wave their arms. Grown men with ordinary jobs suddenly jump to their feet, hooting and hollering and gloating over the vanquished enemy. Little children, following their dads' lead, point jeeringly at the opponents.

Yet we often think heaven will be boring. We see a picture like the one here in Revelation and assume that all the people in heaven will be passive and dull.

Wake up, people! Jesus has defeated sin. Our champion King has disarmed the devil. The Captain of our salvation has knocked even death itself to the ground and will bring victory over death to all who believe. It is better than Stanley Cup, Grey Cup, and FIFA World Series victories all rolled into one.

Eternity will be spent hearing how Jesus won the victory. The parades and celebrations will go on and on as we hear from brothers and sisters throughout the ages: St. Peter and St. Paul, St. Augustine and Mrs. Noah, King David and Ruth, Christians persecuted in China in our times, and those believers who worshiped in secret in the catacombs of Rome centuries ago. We will shout as we learn of people in Africa who survived purges and attacks or were martyred for their faith. We'll hear from believers next door and those separated by centuries, and with each new story we'll shout and stamp our feet and declare, "Holy! Holy! Holy! is the King who leads His people in victory!"

Lord Jesus, Captain of our salvation, stir our souls this day to help us understand the magnitude of the battle raging all around us. Lord of Victory who disarms the enemy, give us a foretaste of the heavenly glory we shall see, hear, feel, smell, and know so intimately so that today we will wake up to the wondrous majesty of who You really are. Forgive us for our tiny, boring view of who You are. Forgive us the times when we are half-asleep and mostly ignorant of all the warfare taking place around us right now. By Your Spirit may we be a people who are more than fans, more than part-time believers, more fully alive and awake and prepared to follow You in the battle that is even now taking place for the souls of men, women, and children. Help us to see how our Father in heaven has planned from the very beginning to pour out His blessings on His people and bring about this great victory parade through His Son. Grant us the great joy of bringing loved ones to Jesus and seeing Him take them from the way of death into the path of foot-stomping, arm-waving, joy-thrilled shouting. Hallelujah to Your name, Crusher of the Enemy, King of Victory! Amen.

DECEMBER 14

Hoya

PREACHING IS SOMETHING I THOROUGHLY ENJOY. HOWEVER, PREACHING TWO services a Sunday can be taxing. This church was my first charge and I didn't have a barrel of sermons to fall back on. When ministers have served in more than one church, they have a lot of sermons prepared on a lot of different scripture passages. Fellow pastors call this their "barrel."

One source of relief was an opportunity I had to go to a church of our denomination that was searching for a pastor. Throughout their search, I was asked every month or two to lead their morning and evening services. During those weeks, I could take a sermon from the barrel and not have to scramble to prepare two new sermons. Between the morning and evening church services, I'd often be billeted at the home of one of the congregation members.

This particular Sunday, I had the great privilege of staying with a family who had just presented their infant son for baptism. Many family members were in the church. A variety of work friends and neighbours of this family crowded into the church to celebrate this joyous day.

After the worship service in which the baptism was celebrated, folks were invited to the large foyer to enjoy a wonderful array of baked goodies and coffee and tea. After much laughter, hand-shaking, and passing around the little lad, he demonstrated the strength of his lungs and screamed and cried with great perseverance. With a squinting of the eyes and a curt nod, the exhausted mom signalled the dad: it was time to go home. The family left with their son and I was invited to spend the rest of the day at their house.

Once the boy was settled in the car, the little guy promptly fell asleep. The peace was so welcome that no one spoke during the car ride, which wended towards the outskirts of town to a new subdivision. John and Barb's modest starter home stood out as one of the first completed homes amid a great mucky mess of clay and snow and loose boards and huge holes ready to receive the pouring of new foundations. With a half-smile of apology, Barb gathered up her baby and noted that the neighbourhood was a disgraceful mess. The driveway, though promised, would not be in place until late spring. "So sorry about your dress shoes," she seemed to say, "but follow me to the house."

As Barb fussed over her son and fed him discretely in one corner of the living room, her husband proudly showed me around the house. It was a treat. He showed the blueprints and improvements he'd made; he had been able to do some of the work himself. Then I followed him into the kitchen where he began preparations for a simple lunch. The soup smelled so good. Especially after sweet baked goods, something a bit more substantial was welcome.

Barb called me out of the kitchen. "Have a seat, pastor, while John pulls the lunch together."

Entering the living room, I saw the little gaffer contentedly asleep in the portable playpen, snuggly wrapped in a blanket. Barb got up and stood nearby after noting that I was admiring a huge hoya plant. There was no greater compliment I could pay her, except of course to remark on the splendid attributes of her dark-haired, rosy-cheeked young lad. She was even more impressed that I knew what the plant was, that it was native to southern India, and that its waxy, deep green leaves and long rope-like leafed trailers could also produce beautiful star-shaped flowers in abundance. The deep colour of the centre of the flower could be as rich a red as you'd find on a Canadian flag. The spray of flowers was so regular and perfect and waxy that lots of folks think they're fake. But oh the smell! In the evening and in the morning, their sweet scent could fill the whole house.

Barb kept nodding and adding little footnotes to my descriptions, which nervousness squeezed out of me. When I'm uncomfortable, I can easily—too easily—spill out all kinds of trivia. But in this instance, Barb was only too happy to listen and supplement. This particular plant was more than thirty years old. The plant always flowered on the old nodes. Her mom had owned it and gotten it to flower profusely. Year in and year out, it would flower for her mom.

When her mom had moved into the retirement home seven years ago, Barb had inherited the plant. Despite proper periods of fertilizing, correctly measured watering times, and the right amount of humidity, this stubborn plant refused to flower for Barb. She was saddened. Though the leaves had variegated speckles, with lapis-lazuli blue dots on many and rich shades of deepest greens on others, though the trailers were full up with nicely shaped and healthy leaves, the plant absolutely, resolutely would not flower. To my chagrin, my suggestions were discarded one by one. All the suggested remedies, and several others I hadn't thought of, had yielded no improvement.

John called from the kitchen. Lunch was ready. Barb called back that she would just wash her hands and be at the table in a couple of minutes. The fan was venting the wonderful smell of soup, so my mouth only started to water when I entered the kitchen.

John apologized. He was very sensitive to strong smells, so the soup would stay on the stove, under the venting hood with the fan on so the rich tomato, basil, and sausage odours wouldn't assault his nose throughout the meal.

Confidently he said that he'd loved the baptism but hated the close crush of people. There were all the smells of aftershave and the hideous blendings of perfumes of all descriptions; his aunty wore an old-fashioned concoction that he was sure he could detect a block away.

Surprised, I blurted out, "How do you cope with Barb's hoya plant? The heady smell must drive you nuts!"

"Oh that." Conspiratorially, he motioned with one hand for me to be quiet. "That cruddy, sickly sweet smell almost killed our dating. When I visited Barb at her mom's place, that stupid plant would make my nose feel like it was bleeding and my brain exploding. When Mom gave Barb that wretched plant, I thought I'd die. But I'm up an hour before Barb every morning, and I faithfully clean the leaves of the plant. Whenever I see the tiniest hint of a new spray of flowers beginning—"

The bathroom door opened. Barb smiled as she came down the hall towards us. While she was still out of earshot and looking past us at her sleeping angel to reassure herself that he'd sleep all through lunch, John whispered just loud enough for me to hear.

"—I simply clip them off before she ever sees them and fold 'em into a tissue and throw them away."

Do you think each spouse knew what the other was doing? Aren't the accommodations we can make for one another great? The King of Glory makes great room for our weaknesses, even as He raises us to maturity in Christ.

> *Don't slip back into your old ways of living to satisfy your own desires... For you have been born again, but not to a life that will quickly end. Your new life will last forever because it comes from the eternal, living word of God.* (1 Peter 1:14, 23)

I laughed quietly as I watched a young couple feed their very young child at a restaurant. It was obvious the baby wasn't used to solid foods, even thoroughly mashed and pureed; she would taste some, then push it out with her lips and tongue. The parents had food all over themselves, not to mention the bib, the high chair, and the floor around the high chair.

We're like that infant. We are so used to our sins and the tawdry, worldly things for which we've acquired a taste that our new life in Christ is a strange sensation. We are inclined to spit out what the Word gives us.

Yet just as those parents persisted, so we need to be persistent. Infancy lasts but a little while, but maturity in Christ will fill our lives here and last forever. We will feast on God's goodness and delight in His presence. Eternity will be tremendous fun, joy, wonder, and laughter. Get a taste for it now in Christ.

> O God, please, so enfold me in Your holy will, that my whole life may be an unfolding of Your purpose concerning me for Jesus' sake.
> —Mary Wilder Tileston (adapted)

DECEMBER 15

Epic Gagging

A YOUNG FAMILY HAD BEFRIENDED US. THROUGH COFFEE CHATS AND CASUAL visits, our six children came to realize that all of us thoroughly enjoyed *Star Wars*. The suggestion was made that on the school break (which we always called the Christmas break though politically correct lunkheads call it the holiday break) our families would get together and watch all three original *Star Wars* episodes—*Star Wars*, and then *The Empire Strikes Back*, and final *The Return of the Jedi*. What a night it would be.

The idea took off and watching the trilogy became an annual tradition for our two families. One of those traditional gatherings has, in our family folklore, become as known as the "*Star Wars* incident."

Since this took place in the depths of a prairie winter and the best TV for viewing the movies was in the basement, it took a lot of arranging, pillows, blankets, and arguing in order to get everyone situated and in comfortable reach of all the assorted snacks and drinks available for the children. The adults sat and sort of watched the movies while engaging in conversation or a rousing game of hand-and-foot canasta.

Undersupervised, the younglings gorged. Our youngest, Elayna, had managed to get the bowl of cheese puffs. These pseudo-cheese snacks came in long sleeves and the snacks were a brilliant hue of orange. Elayna merrily munched and filled in the tiny crevices of her stomach with pop.

As the card game ended and the movie hit a particularly appealing point, the four adults drifted back and confiscated the best seats—the couches. The children reluctantly settled on the floor. Oblivious, Elayna softly sucked in air and dozed a bit restlessly. She was squeezed in between the legs of the coffee table and the couch. She scrunched as comfortably as she could on the white shag carpet. Then, like the slight twitches of the tip of a fishing rod when a fish nibbles below, her stomach made a quick heaving movement.

The movement caught Mom's eye. "She's gonna blow!"

That was all she had time to say before a cheesy eruption of vomit projected a few feet before cascading down her face, down her long dark blonde hair. Finally the lava-like puke pooled and swished through the white shag carpet. Mom juggled a nearly empty bowl to catch the final soggy, sticky regurgitated remains swirling around Elayna's mouth and face. She swept her little girl up as the caterwauling began; our little one had begun vomiting while asleep, so the heaving and sour tastes had awakened and frightened her at the same time. Off to the tub she was carried.

Meanwhile, unmoved in the least, three boys remained glued to the big TV and watched the familiar scenes of space fighters and explosions. The two remaining girls and I began the task of cleaning. No matter how much water and mild soap we raked through the areas where the throw-up had flowed, the orange tinge could never quite be removed.

As the final credits rolled, our oldest son's eyes swept across the couch, strewn pop bottles, empty cups, and soppy shag carpet.

"You missed a spot," he helpfully noted. "I'll bet that orange colour will never leave that carpet."

Great. Thanks, son.

He was right. It never did. A hurried ending to our marathon became a family legend, funnier and grosser in the retelling. Thankfully, our friends have a great sense of humour and we are friends still.

CAN'T HELP MYSELF

Sometimes all we remember are the little Sunday School children we had around our ankles. We forget that these little ones grow bigger than our stories of their childhood, and become men and women who work for the Kingdom.

> *It is not by force nor by strength, but by my Spirit, says the LORD of Heaven's Armies. Nothing, not even a mighty mountain, will stand in Zerubbabel's way; it will become a level plain before him! And when Zerubbabel sets the final stone of the Temple in place, the people will shout: "May God bless it! May God bless it!" …Do not despise these small beginnings, for the LORD rejoices to see the work begin…* (Zechariah 4:6–7, 10)

Zerubbabel, one of Jesus' ancestors, was the leader of a people newly returned from exile. The people had been sent into exile because of their sins.

> Repentance always precedes rejoicing. God is knocking at the door of the church as the Divine Disturber, and we've got "Do Not Disturb" signs on our door.
>
> Here we are in the twenty-first century, upset because of the cultural decay. We bemoan the policies of Washington (Ottawa) but do not rebuke the backslidden in our churches. We complain about the prevalence of worldly thinking and its effect on the family, but the family of God has divorced itself from the Father. We have more prodigals than prophets.[4]
> —Michael Catt

Yet those who live in the strength of the Spirit of Jesus Christ take a stand against the corruption of the world. Those who make a beginning in His holiness bring forth the rejoicing of the Lord, and the hearts of others who see it are stirred to praise.

Rather than wringing your hands this day at the corruption and brokenness of our world, fold your hands and pray for the Divine Disturber to come and bring His change in you and your world.

ALMIGHTY God, Giver of all good, Who hast given, above all Thy gifts, the crowning mercy that we are called in Christ

---

[4] Michael Catt, *The Power of Surrender* (Nashville, TN: B&H Publishing Group, 2010), 272–273.

Jesus to know and love and serve Thee, we would bring Thee thanks and praises for the Divine Light which reveals the heart of grace in Thy leading of souls and peoples. Help us to rise to a fit gratitude for the overrunning blessings which Thou givest ever, even to the darkest lot in life,—the temporal felicities, the Divine comforts, the eternal hopes. That all things are of Thy mercy, by Thy mercy, and in Thy mercy, we thank Thee. Make us to sing Thy song in the light, and in the night to touch Thy hand and be at peace. Grant, we pray, with all other blessings, Thy best gift, thankful and trustful hearts, that Thou mayest be our Lord and King for evermore—Amen.
—Henry Foote (1838–1889)

DECEMBER 16

Proper Tithe

KEN LIVES ON IN MEMORY AS ONE OF THE MOST HANDSOME MEN I'VE MET, BUT that is not what grabbed my attention at our first meeting. He was also one of the most godly men I've met.

The elders and deacons of our congregation had met, and after a series of discussions they decided it would not be good for me, their young pastor in his first charge, to attend the ministerial meetings any longer.

"Pastor," they said, "who knows what kinds of heresy you may pick up by going there?"

"Who knows what blessings of the Reformed faith I might be able to shed abroad at such meetings," I replied feebly. It was met with suppressed laughter by one highly embarrassed elder, and stern looks by the others.

It was decided. I could not be a member of the evangelical ministerial association.

Before this had taken place at, and shortly after my first few meetings with the evangelical ministerial association, Ken had approached me and asked who I prayed with on a regular basis. He was surprised that I had not yet found a prayer partner in the city. He offered to meet with me. And so it was, on Friday mornings, from 10:00 a.m. until 11:30 or so, we'd meet one week at my church and the following week at his home or at his church and we'd pray.

During the course of those meetings, we learned more about the other's denomination. On the rare Sunday that one of us was free from preaching responsibilities, we would visit the other's church. Ken was fascinated that our services began with "God's Greeting," usually the words of greeting such as can be found at the start of most of the New Testament letters. The worship service would end with a blessing, "God's Blessing"—again, words which could be found at the end of New Testament letters or in such places as Numbers 6:24–26 (which he soon learned was my favourite blessing to speak over the flock the Lord had given me to serve).

His worship services were much more free-flowing. There were no bulletins or any discernible order to the service. People would get up and pray, or sing, or all would sing, and at some point my friend would preach. He had a deep baritone voice, and a great ability to weave an interesting story as he preached. The word would go out with power among his people, many of whom were very poor, restless, and driven by addictions which made sitting for long periods of time difficult—but Ken's voice would keep them still.

Besides comparing the way in which our worship services were conducted, we also compared our job descriptions. Ken was part of the Pentecostal Church, and I wasn't sure what to expect. My Reformed tradition had rules governing all kinds of things. He read and then reread my job description. I wasn't sure what he was looking for, specifically, until I saw his job description. Near the top, after the preamble which highlighted his call to service, there was in print the expectation that he would tithe his time in prayer.

Even as I write this story now, more than twenty years later, I am still moved by the vision of this job description and the spiritual poverty in my own job description.

Is my denomination or local congregation the only one which has the truth? It is important for us as Christians to know our own strengths and weaknesses, even as we evaluate what we perceive to be the strengths and weaknesses of those who share our faith but have a different emphasis.

> *I said to myself, "I will watch what I do and not sin in what I say. I will hold my tongue when the ungodly are around me." But as I stood there in silence—not even speaking of good things—the turmoil within me grew worse. The more I thought about it, the hotter I got, igniting a fire of words: "LORD, remind me how brief my time on earth will be. Remind me that my days are numbered—how fleeting my life is. You have made my life no longer than the width of my hand. My entire lifetime is just a moment to you; at best, each of us is but a breath."* (Psalm 39:1–5)

The more I think about it—the goodness of God, the depths of my forgiveness, the sure hope we have in Christ, how awesome it is to belong to the people of God, how many people all around us need to know His goodness—the hotter I get, igniting a fire of words.

Isn't that true? It is impossible to keep quiet about the greatness of our God! It's like a fire that builds up inside which must be expressed.

Life is short; tell others of God's goodness. Life is brief; clear up the accounts of others' wrongdoing. In light of God's glory and grace, find your way to offering and receiving forgiveness in Christ. Today is Sunday; get to church. Get together with the people of God. Shalom.

God, You sent Your Spirit as tongues of fire on that first Pentecost. Bless Your people now so that same Spirit will once again ignite within us all the fires of renewed devotion to Jesus and greater kindness to others. In Jesus' Name we pray, amen.

DECEMBER 17

Cold Fridays

ONE OF THE HARDEST THINGS OUR FAMILY HAD TO ADJUST TO WHILE WE LIVED out in the prairies was the cold that would drive deep into our bones. My small group leader would say, "Yes, but the flu bugs are killed by this kind of cold." This is little comfort when your lips are bleeding from being so painfully chapped. Or someone might say, "It is cold, but it's a dry cold. Not like the Ontario cold that is damp." To which all I could exclaim is, "You're kidding me, right?"

When the temperature plunges below −25 degrees Celsius, the water vapour in the air freezes and forms little ice particles that dance in the air and drift down. −25 is −25 no matter where you are, and there seems to be no way to get comfortable. One of the great pleasures I had was to snuggle down under many blankets on a Friday evening and watch a movie with the kids as we ate pizza—or, after they'd gone to bed, I'd watch a movie with Carolyn.

Of course, my friend Ken would mess with all of that.

"This is a big town," he'd say. "There are so many people who are hungry and cold. Join me as we hand out coffee and sandwiches around the downtown."

He'd repeat variations on this over the weeks. I'd just shake my head. My conscience was messing with me so I didn't trust my voice to give a firm enough no in reply.

Finally, Ken looked me in the eye one day and said, "Brother, here we are praying for the people of our city. We are praying for their salvation. We are praying they will experience the love of God. How will they know it if we don't show it?"

I could offer no adequate rebuttal if I intended to keep praying with him. He wasn't trying to guilt me and he wasn't trying to pressure me. He showed me the power of prayer: God will move hearts and hands, and wallets (my own included), in response to prayer.

Those Friday morning prayer times softened my heart. My respect for Ken was such that I had to go with him. His final advice: "Dress really, really warm."

With a double set of long johns, double mittens inside a pair of leather gloves, and a scarf to wrap around my face, I figured I was ready. What caused me to shiver wasn't the cold, but how poorly dressed the first few people who met our bus were. The bus had sandwiches and hot chocolate and hot coffee and the people who came by that night were all shades of red from the cold. Worse, they were turning white from the cold and frostbite was close.

Sheltered as I had been, I had no idea how to respond to the language of the street people. Whereas the cold produced diamond-like ice crystals that caught the light, the language of the people seemed to me to produce droplets of suspended faecal syllables that I hardly dared pass through. I would stop in place. I'd step back. It was involuntary, because I'd never been exposed to F-bombs used like simple punctuation.

To my lasting shame, my participation in those cold Friday nights was very infrequent. My respect for my colleague grew and, looking back now, I realize that God was preparing me for the day and time when my ministerial calling would be to people very much like these, who didn't worry about what words were used around them; they were desperate for food and something warm.

Little did I realize how much my heart needed to grow. Little did I realize how much I'd ignored the needs of the people who lived in my town and crowded the doorways and any little patch which might afford protection from the wind, a bit of warmth to ward off the cold of the night. Little did I realize how I preached love but still had to learn how to demonstrate it among those who most needed it.

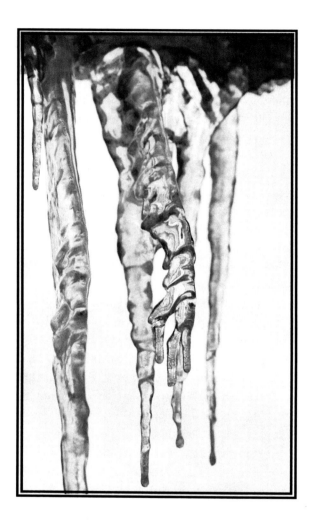

Things or people? Too often we are attached to things in our lives precious things, but we neglect the more important focus: the people God has placed in our path, our city, and our world.

> *Do not withhold good from those to whom it is due, when it is in your power to act. Do not say to your neighbor, "Come back tomorrow and I'll give it to you"—when you already have it with you.* (Proverbs 3:27–28, NIV)

Hmm. Who do you think is good enough to "deserve" your kindness? It is much easier to hunker down under a warm blanket with a bowl of popcorn and a good movie than it is to go out and exercise your power to do good. That is the point of God's grace. While we were yet sinners, Christ died for us, removing the curse God has placed on sin. He showed kindness and love when we did not deserve it. This is a powerful call to act with kindness beyond anyone's deserving. This passage from Proverbs calls for us to build community in Jesus' Name.

> O LORD, my God, Fountain of all true and holy love; who has made me, and preserved me, that I might love Thee; give to Thy servant such a love, that whatsoever in Thy service may happen contrary to flesh and blood, I may not feel it; that humility may be my sanctuary, and Thy service the joy of my soul, and death, itself the entrance of an eternal life, when I may live with Thee, my Strength, and my Refuge, my God and everlasting Hope—Amen.
> —Jeremy Taylor (1613–1667)

DECEMBER 18

Uncle Izaak

WE CALLED HIM OOM IET, WHICH IS PRONOUNCED "OHM EAT." *OOM* MEANS uncle; Iet is the nickname used by our Dutch family in the Netherlands. My mother was the youngest of seven children and Oom Iet was the youngest son, the sixth child. His wife didn't like to travel and was afraid of flying, so Oom Iet would visit us periodically with his sister, Tante Rie (*tante* is the Dutch word for aunt, and Rie is the nickname for Maria). Tante Rie had been widowed and the two of them got along very well. Oom Iet's wife, Tante Flora, would take biking holidays in the Netherlands when he travelled to Canada to visit us.

He was hard of hearing and funny. He had a special place in my sister's heart, and when my daughter was born, his heart grew and added room for Elayna. He was so kind and always had a special *knuffle* for her. I've never exactly understood what the word *knuffle* means. If I remember my Dutch correctly, a *knufflebeest* is a cuddly toy or a stuffed bear. I guess it makes sense. Our little Elayna would jump into his arms and he would hug her and give her a single kiss on her forehead.

One winter, while we were in our prairie charge, Oom Iet (now widowed and bereft of his sister, Rie) decided he would come to Canada and visit us. So my parents and uncle took the train from Burlington to the prairies. Understand this: the Netherlands has an excellent train service. Granted, it is a very small country and trains are very convenient. Canadian trains seem to have to wait for freight cars and all manner of things, so the train was late in arriving by hours and hours. In fact, around 4:00 a.m., I had to get to the train station, the brutal cold seeming to frost the breath before it left my mouth.

Oom Iet was ready to talk as soon as the trio arrived. He lifted his luggage from the train platform into the van, which thankfully did start that deeply cold morning. We went to a coffee shop. Amazed, my uncle asked, "Is it open *now?*" Of course. And so it was, in the biting depths of winter, that I was seated with my dad, my mom, and my uncle in a coffee shop at 4:30 a.m.

He was somewhat deaf, having served in the Indonesian War where the gunfire had damaged her hearing. He walked with a cane. He always had a walking cap as well, and from what I learned years afterwards, he would ride his bike great distances even when his walking had become terribly unsure; his ability to stay on a bike and keep his balance was undiminished. It was impressive.

Oom Iet was a short man. He got along famously with my mom. Mom, Dad, and Iet genuinely loved one another. In the evenings, they'd share a *borreltje* (a shot of a strong drink) and the stories would unfold. He had a quiet dignity about him as well, which made his affection for our daughter all the sweeter. They couldn't communicate with one another, because his English was terrible and her ability to speak or understand Dutch non-existent.

My mom had knit sweaters for our boys; they were white sweaters with a design of handprints on them. Elayna received a pretty dress. So it made sense for us all to have family pictures taken. That was a throwback to the posed pictures of yesteryear, when great gobs of extended family would visit and we'd go to a photographer in order to have portraits taken. A lady from the congregation was a very well-known photographer and the resulting portraits are, to this day, a beautiful record of a fine visit.

The deep snow, pervasive cold, and short winter days fascinated Oom Iet. We regularly walked, even on days when the thermometer plunged below −25 degrees. He loved seeing the local cemetery, one of the oldest in the region. There'd be little grave markers for infants. Sometimes the cause of death was listed as influenza. Other times there'd be a little information beyond the sad record: "Lived four days." One gravestone noted a much-loved husband who was lost in a snowstorm and left behind his wife and family. Oom Iet would then share a memory of our own family. Since my mother was the youngest by a number of years, she doesn't have near the storehouse of memory about extended family as did Oom Iet.

My parents had decided to pick up some groceries and do a bit of shopping, which we knew could last for hours. We were not surprised. Our busy house with three children could be incredibly loud for their tastes, since they'd been empty nesters for years already. Oom Iet donned his walking cap and picked up the cane. He was determined to walk. It was cold, even by prairie standards, and I tried to dissuade him. It was Saturday and the next day I'd have to preach twice. Being relatively new in the pastorate and having company eat up a lot of my time meant that I was going to be tied to my study and practicing sermons in order to be prepared for Sunday.

I can still see him trudging away through the drifting snow. He shrugged his shoulders a few times, as if trying to extract warmth from his coat and adjust it in order to better snuggle into it and be protected from the wind. It was supposed to be a short walk, just fifteen minutes or so in order "to get a fresh nose." Apparently that Dutch expression made sense to Oom Iet, but it baffled me.

When half an hour had elapsed and there was no sign of Oom Iet, and the prairie day was drawing to its early dusk, I started pacing. What would I tell my parents? Um, I lost Oom Iet? I could imagine his taking a place next to that other prairie wanderer who a century before had lost his way in the cold. What kind of daft nephew was I to leave him to walk alone?

Forty minutes crept by. My parents had the family car for their shopping trip. I couldn't even drive out to try and find him.

More than forty-five minutes passed and I was at the point of calling the police. Unreasonable fears and grotesque imaginings took hold of me. Even my children were beginning to see the way in which I was radiating fear and concern. They started acting out.

Suddenly the back door opened. Oom Iet walked in, nearly frozen, his olive skin now patchy white in places. We got him peeled out of his overcoat and scarf and prepared a hot coffee. We gave him the warmest place in the house and a blanket, and Elayna snuggled in his arms with an innocence that seemed to will warmth into his bones.

In quiet, quick Dutch, my uncle spoke. No doubt he'd heard the loud squeaking of the garage as my parents returned home. His glance confirmed his suspicion that I was terrified at facing my parents and having to confess something like, "I almost killed Oom Iet by letting him walk alone in the dreadful cold of this day."

"Ree-shart,[5] der is no need to talk about dis," Oom Iet said. "All is fine."

At this moment, I realized that my Oom Iet was not frail as I'd always thought him to be. I had been fooled by the cane and deafness. This experience showed me a depth of humanity I had never really credited to any person of my parents' generation.

Sometimes a moment's experience can so infiltrate the heart that years of pondering and reflection afterwards only enriches the understanding and signals how complex and marvellous is our shared humanity. I have much yet to learn.

---

[5] Richard is, to this day, pronounced "Ree-shart" by my parents and assorted Dutch relatives.

[King] Joash did what was right in the eyes of the LORD all the years Jehoiada the priest instructed him. (2 Kings 12:2, NIV)

A good mentor is a powerful gift from God. Joash was very young when he became king over Judah, and as long as the elderly priest mentored him, he was faithful to the Lord. All of us need mentors, more mature brothers and sisters in Christ who can speak into our lives, who can get past our defenses and teach us. In His great kindness and love, our Father in heaven appoints people to help us at various stages and times in our lives. Will you listen to their good instruction and put it into practice? And when the Spirit provides the chance, will you offer yourself as a mentor to others who might need help readjusting the course of their lives? It is both a great privilege and hard work.

Lord, You are the God who leads those who have gone astray. In Your great kindness and love, You provide mentors and leaders, ministers and teachers, kindly family members and friends in order to bring us to the right path. When we are called to be students, help us to be humble learners. When You give us the opportunity to mentor others, may we do so with the gentleness of the Great Shepherd of the sheep. Amen.

DECEMBER 19

Micah's Healing

A SMALL GROUP FROM THE CHURCH WOULD MEET CAROLYN AND MYSELF AT least once a month. Their purpose was to support us through prayer, scripture, hospitality, and when necessary advocacy to the church board or committees. What a funny group they were. What intimacy we shared.

One summer, we travelled to Ontario visit our family. Since I had a limited number of vacation days, Carolyn stayed a bit longer with the children in order to attend a friend's wedding and have some time with her parents. Carolyn's parents, Oma and Opa with the pipe, were great at including the children in all their activities. Opa was out cutting wood with a chainsaw and Micah was given a hacksaw and allowed to cut whatever branches he wanted. It was heaven for him.

No one is quite sure what happened that morning, but by the evening, Micah's eye had swollen nearly shut. Increasingly he began to complain of pain. Unsure what was going on, Carolyn's dad drove her and Micah to the emergency room. Micah was attended to almost immediately and soon thereafter admitted to the paediatrics ward.

There were concerns for his eye. He was a little tyke and IV antibiotics were necessary in order to fight the infection. But the nurse couldn't find a vein. The IV needle was inserted into his temple. It looked so strange, Carolyn reported; I only heard second-hand. We were too poor to afford me traveling to Ontario to be there.

One of the ladies on our pastoral care small group had an open door policy. She usually had some scrumptious baked goodie or another at hand. It was early evening and I drifted there. She was just a bit older than my mother and it was reassuring to be able to go to her and pour out my heart.

Oddly enough, she didn't speak much. She kept knitting as I spoke, the needles clacking and ticking in irregular rhythm as she worked the unusual pattern. When the torrent of my words ended, there was intermittent silence. Just the soft clatter of the needles and an occasional hiss in the direction of the cat who was too interested in the unravelling ball of yarn.

Into that space she observed, "You know, I never voted for you to be our minister."

I almost choked. It was said without malice or much emotion. Her fingers still deftly looped the yarn over one needle as the other caught it and wove it into place.

I knew the vote for me had been nearly unanimous. I couldn't imagine why someone who hadn't voted for me would then be part of my pastoral team, which was supposed to encourage me. Is this what encouragement was supposed to look like?

The pause lengthened into increasingly awkward silence. This woman, who usually spoke Dutch, was obviously grasping deep into her treasury of English words and phrases in order to carefully state what had been impressed on her heart.

"It was not my first choice to have you here," she said. "I thought we needed a man wid experience in ministry and de skills dat come wid long service in order to lead us."

Not an encouraging start.

She sighed, unconsciously shuffling her foot in the direction of the cat in order to distract him from his intended pounce on the yarn. Her knitting needles fell silent. As her hands dropped to her lap, still holding the tension on the yarn, the needles formed an "x," with the pointed ends spearing the space between us.

"I was not wrong. Experience is goed." She examined the pattern, making sure it conformed to the instructions she knew by heart. "But

I also know that our plans are not God's. What He does wve don't understant."

She nodded and smiled to herself, an action which I realized was not so much meant to encourage me as show her relief that the stitch count was correct.

The coffee was cold now. She set the handwork aside. Looking directly at me, she offered a brief, sincere prayer.

I suddenly found myself standing on the front porch as the long day drew around it a beautiful multihued mantle of sunset.

It took me many days of reflection to figure out what it all meant. Despite her not voting for me, she was supportive. Despite the fact that things don't turn out as we expect, God is in charge. What a great lesson, strangely given.

Oh! As for Micah, he never pulled at his IV needle. Many children see it on their arm or hand and pull at it. Micah couldn't see it. Didn't pull at it. He ate piles and piles of banana-flavoured popsicles. And the IV antibiotics did their work. His eye healed completely.

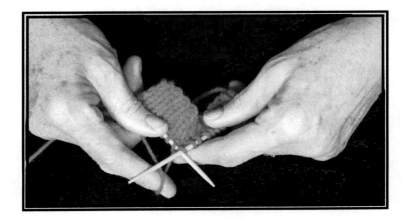

God cares for the humble, for those who are aware of their need for His gracious presence. The ways in which He makes us humble... well, that's where the previous story enters the picture for me. Humility, for some of us, is a lesson about which we will need regular refreshers.

> *Though the LORD is great, he cares for the humble, but he keeps his distance from the proud. Though I am surrounded by troubles, you will protect me from the anger of my enemies. You reach out your hand, and the power of your right hand saves me.* (Psalm 138:6–7)

Have you ever felt God has forgotten you? Have you ever found yourself on the backside of the desert? Did you have high aspirations for your life only to discover life as not turned out like you thought it would? Have you convinced yourself that your failure is final? It doesn't have to be. Brokenness can lead to blessings. Abandonment to your plans can position you to follow God's plans.

As long as you think you can help God out, you can't be what God wants you to be. Revival is not about helping God out; it's about surrender and abandonment. It may be that time has not passed you by but that you've been running ahead of God. You need to turn aside and get alone with Him.[6]

—Michael Catt

O BLESSED Lord, who hast commanded us to love another, grant us grace that, having received Thine undeserved bounty, we may love every one in Thee and for Thee. We implore Thy clemency for all; but especially for the friends whom Thy love has given to us. Love Thou them, O Thou Fountain of love, and make them to love Thee with all their heart, that they may will, and speak, and do those things only which are pleasing to Thee—Amen.

—St. Anselm (1033–1109)

---

[6] Michael Catt, *The Power of Surrender* (Nashville, TN: B&H Publishing Group, 2010), 239.

DECEMBER 20

Heaping Christmas

CAROLYN AND I ALWAYS STRUGGLED WITH HOW MUCH TO SPEND ON OUR children for Christmas. If we bought a lot, then the omas and opas were the wildcard. Some years it seemed as if the omas and opas were in collusion and we'd have way more gifts than was healthy for our little ones. Other years there'd be a chocolate letter from each set of grandparents and from us as parents, but little else from them and there'd be no explanation as to why.

We did not want to instill in our children a spirit of consumerism and greed. Instead we wanted to nurture and grow young hearts which beat in gratitude to God.

When I was in seminary, one of the requirements for graduation was to have a one-year placement in a church. Well, the first round of interviews took place and no church offered my wife and I an internship. The second round of interviews took place and still nothing. I remember walking down the hallway in the seminary and trying to hold it all together when suddenly I saw my prayer partner, Tim. I burst into tears. Exactly as a prayer partner should, he gathered me in his arms, briefly held me tight, and then most importantly led me to Jesus' throne of grace. He prayed. I'll never forget it.

What a great gift it was to receive a quick answer to that prayer. The Director of Field Education at seminary tracked me down and mentioned that there was a church which hadn't yet received a student placement. The student they'd selected had a few choices of other placements and hadn't chosen to go to this particular church in a rural town in the San Joaquin Valley of California. A few days and a successful interview later, we knew we'd be heading to California in six months. Carolyn confessed it had been her dream as a child to live in California. We'd be living the dream.

Sure enough, it was delight. The church was very large and there were great opportunities to be trained in all aspects of ministry. I fondly remember the pastor who mentored me. He was very keen on visiting his people, and I learned all about the best ways to offer pastoral care in hospital visits, sick visits, wellness visits, casual drop-in visits, and how to follow up with people who were on the way out of church and how to gently try to draw them back. The church responded well to our ministry and was stoically kind when some of the sermons I'd laboured over were flops and painful exercises in listening.

One kindly old soul came up to me in December, after six months of this internship, and said, "I don't remember a single sermon you preached here, but that children's message you gave on that last Sunday in September I'll never forget."

He smiled broadly and walked away.

At the time, I wasn't sure if he'd never forget it because it was so good in contrast to all the sermons I had preached, or worse, he'd never forget it because it stood out as the worst children's message he'd ever heard. Remembering his broad, exaggerated smile, I decided it was the former rather than the latter… and then I had a twinge of self-doubt, thinking, *That's better, right?*

Since this was an internship, we were paid a reasonable amount, but it was not generous. Christmas presented some challenges with regards to what we could afford. So Carolyn and I determined how much—actually, how little—we'd be spending. Since Adrian and Micah were so young, we decided to limit it to one larger gift and one smaller gift. Garage sale items were not out of the question, and the beautiful California weather meant even December could yield some treasures to grab a toddler's attention on Christmas morning.

However, it was not to be. Fully ten days before Christmas, our doorbell started ringing with unexpected guests. First, there was a young couple who'd befriended us right at the start of this internship. They came with two gifts for each of the boys. Suddenly we had four gifts for each of them.

That same afternoon, a couple who at the time were the same age as our parents came for a coffee visit, and they also brought a laundry basket half full of gifts for our children. We were embarrassed and touched. How could we accept such extravagance? Their answer: "We know you are far from home and it is our pleasure to treat you like one of our children for a season."

Then the almond farmers came with variety packs of delicious California almonds. Ranchers came with beef for our freezer. A whole host of people of various ages came as surrogate uncles and aunts and gave more and more gifts.

Sitting in our living room, we would shake our heads as we saw the tree which had gifts right up to the lowest branches; it almost made it seem that the tree was sitting on top of gifts. Piled behind the tree were still more gifts. You could see the sparkle of gold and blue, silver and red, from the wrapping paper peeking through the branches of the tree. It was an explosion of gifts.

When we started unwrapping on Christmas morning, we soon realized that the boys were overwhelmed. We had to stop unwrapping after a while and go and play with some of the gifts and take a walk; they just couldn't unwrap another gift.

On day two, we opened a whole pile of gifts so that it no longer looked as if the tree was propped up. But once again, the heaping pile of gifts proved too much for young, excited hands and hearts. The boys started getting distracted and fidgety. They wanted to play with the gifts they'd received rather than open more. So we called a halt to the shredding, tearing, and ripping-open bonanza.

On day three, we paced ourselves a bit, and with exhausted wonder opened the final offerings of that "Heaping Christmas." I cannot even recall any of the gifts our children received. What I do remember is an outpouring of love from a congregation that put up with a young intern pastor, his wife, and his children, and demonstrated their love in the best way they knew.

Sometimes a minister will complain, "I live in a glass house. Everything I do is scrutinized and judged and weighed by the congregation." It might be true. But I remember with thanks before God how He provided a job with such flexibility that my wife and I can attend our children's school performances during the day.

Part of our job is visiting people and sharing their joys. Part of the job is being invited into times of sickness and sorrow and having the privilege of communicating the loving presence of our God and King. And there is, in the background, the memory of the Heaping Christmas. Surely we have experienced the kindness of our King through His people.

CAN'T HELP MYSELF

What is it you are called to surrender to the Lord? What are you withholding that is in your power to give? How easily do you receive gifts from others when you're not in a position to give a gift in return?

> *Then the LORD sent this message through the prophet Haggai: "Why are you living in luxurious houses while my house lies in ruins? This is what the LORD of Heaven's Armies says: Look at what's happening to you! You have planted much but harvest little. You eat but are not satisfied. You drink but are still thirsty. You put on clothes but cannot keep warm. Your wages disappear as though you were putting them in pockets filled with holes!"* (Haggai 1:3–6)

The first protest you might feel in reading this prophecy is, "My house is not luxurious!" Right. In a world where a billion or more people live on a dollar per day or less, having food, shelter, and clothing means you are living in luxury. More than that, how many of you reading this are running around buying gifts you can't afford for people in your life? So you are willing to spend yourself into debt, which is a form of idolatry, but you are not willing to tithe to the living God as true worship. You are willing to pour your energy into your hobbies, but you are not willing to attend God's house and worship with His people. You are willing to bring your kids to hockey, to soccer, to dance, or to whatever activity, but you are not training them to honour God above all else by keeping the appointed times for worship.

The Lord invites us to test Him on this. Prepare to make a New Year's resolution: this will be the year that you renew your vows to be truly faithful to God, to get back to church, to be involved, to give of your time, treasures, and talents, and see how the Lord will give you great satisfaction in serving Him.

> O Almighty God, who alone can order the unruly wills and affections of sinful men and sinful women, grant to Your people that they may love the thing which You command, and desire that which You promise, that so, among the sundry and manifold changes of the world, our hearts may surely there be fixed, where true joys are to be found: through Jesus Christ our Lord.[7]

---

[7] There are many variations of this prayer. Near as I can find, there are two main sources for this particular version: the Gelasian Prayer of 492 and Gregorian Book of Common Prayer. 590.

DECEMBER 21

O Holy Night

MY FAVOURITE CHRISTMAS CAROL IS ONE I WAS LARGELY UNFAMILIAR WITH FOR many years. Even though the carol is more than a hundred years old, I wasn't exposed to it in the church where I grew up.

The days marched closer and closer to Christmas and I struggled to find the right words to speak to my congregation. Christmas Eve and Christmas Day were always celebrated with great vigour and full attendance. Even people who had intermittent attendance during the year would make an extra special effort to attend these services. So the pressure was on, and the more pressure I felt, the less likely it was that I could form a coherent sentence reflecting on the assigned text.

Part of the difficulty is that the story is already so familiar—the text is so familiar, and the whole service and how it progresses so familiar—and I believe people come to church at Christmas wanting to hear something new.

There was a hymn we sang often in the church of my youth: "Tell me the old, old story of Jesus and His glory, of Jesus and His love." The problem was that the pacing of the hymn was so slow, and the people singing it never seemed to reflect either the glory or extravagant love of this supposedly wonderful Saviour. This experience seemed to pinpoint exactly what was wrong: the old, old story was tired and people weren't singing it with the breathless wonder or expectant joy which ought to have been woven throughout. They were singing it knowing that the end of the service was near and half-salivating because there'd be a Sunday dinner waiting for them at home.

Hmm, I felt that same way about the Christmas service I was to prepare. It felt like people would attend it as the prerequisite to enjoying a gut-busting, sleep-coma-inducing turkey dinner, along with wide-reaching desserts and sweets to add to their already over-expanded waistline.

Then I had a quiet moment of awakening. It wasn't so much about the people of the congregation, the regulars and those who only attended a few times a year. This was about my own heart, squeezed dry. Yet I was required to preach and point to Him who is living water for the soul.

It was late already and Carolyn and the children had gone to bed many hours before. So I wandered from the study to the kitchen. There was nothing I wanted to eat. Back to the study. Then to the bathroom. I was about to drift to the kitchen again and instead decided to watch some TV.

A station was broadcasting Mass with all the vestments and ritual that look so impressive. But it didn't keep my attention long. I turned to the music channel, which was just coming out of commercials. The singer—obviously a country singer, given his hat and blue jeans—stood in front of a deep blue background and a bright, exaggerated star shining above. Some wooden planks were constructed in such a way as to evoke the stable of the first Christmas night.

I took it all in, and then his deep voice began: "O holy night, the stars are brightly shining."

His voice was deep honey and gin, smooth and biting, the words electric for my soul. There were no cutaways, no flashing of many images like so many other music videos. The simplicity allowed the viewer-listener to concentrate on the words and the clear deep timbre of the voice.

Here was the old, old story told in such a way as to open the storehouse of refreshment. The first tear formed at the edge of my eye, and the ones that followed didn't so much drench my shirt as flow inwards and water my soul.

For many days and Christmases afterwards, I would scan the music channel to find that particular rendition of "O Holy Night," but I have never seen it again. I don't know the artist's name. It lingers in memory: the simplicity of the set and the power of the words, the song, and the old, old story.

It occurs to me that repeating stories of family events binds us together. As people shake their heads and chuckle, one voice might begin, "Remember this uncle and how he'd always whistle when he was happy?" Another might chime in, "Remember Aunty's potato salad, and how yellow it was and how she'd make designs with green pepper rings and them clever-cut radishes?" In learning the stories, the little ones might begin to see their place in it. The older ones welcome the younger ones. All take their turns with "remember when" stories, followed by laughter. There'd be knockoffs of favourite dishes and new undiscovered favourites.

One Christmas so long ago, a heart squeezed dry by the relentless tide of required sermons suddenly experienced a storm in the desert, resulting in blossoms in the wilderness.

Most people didn't notice. Oddly enough, the highest acknowledgement came from my wife. While most people passing from the sanctuary to the stairway will shake my hand, she often pauses awkwardly. We've already said good morning. She is not physically expressive and doesn't care for handshakes and hugs. People near her in line smirk and wait to see how Carolyn will walk past me towards the stairs and the coffee urns.

This particular Christmas, there was no levity, no awkwardness. She paused directly in front of me and said, "Thank you."

Those nearby didn't understand. "Thank you" for what? I knew. It was for a sermon and a service delivered from a well-watered soul.

One hymn declares, "I love to tell the story!" Sometimes we need to turn to the well of living water before we can jubilantly declare this wonderful story.

*I said to the L*ORD*, "You are my God!"*
*Listen, O L*ORD*, to my cries for mercy!*
*O Sovereign L*ORD*, the strong one who rescued me,*
you protected me in the day of battle. (Psalm 140:6–7)

BE Thou favourable unto me, merciful, sweet and gracious Lord, and grant to me, Thy poor, needy creature, sometimes at least to feel if it be but a small portion of Thy hearty affectionate love; that my faith may become more strong, my hope in Thy goodness may be increased, and that love, once kindled within me, may never fail—Amen.
—Thomas À Kempis (1379–1471)

DECEMBER 22

Pee

WILHELMINA MOANED SOFTLY IN HER NURSING HOME BED. TO MY YOUTHFUL eyes, she looked like a great lumpy mass of flesh and mismatched clothing. When she caught the movement of her dominee entering the room, the moaning ceased immediately. It wasn't until long years afterwards that I realized how great her pain really was, the number of things her aging body coped with, the intensity of her back and bone issues, and whatever else ailed her. All these things she wanted to hide from me.

Forgive me, dear old parishioner, for my impatient visits. Forgive me for the times I wanted to run home at the end of the day and play with my children. The standing rule was I'd be home around 4:30 p.m., and from then until around 7:30 I'd hang out with my children and eat supper with them. Sometimes we'd play Monopoly. Other times we'd build a Lego tower using all of our blocks until they reached the ceiling. Then, if it didn't fall on its own, one of the kids would try to knock it while I tried to block and soon we'd be in a wrestling match. They were so full of life and vigour.

What a contrast to this visit.

Once I asked her, "Wilhelmina, how long have you struggled with it? The pain, I mean?"

"Wvhen I wvas a little girl, I askt my mudder about it. She told me it vood pass before I become an olt man." Seeing my surprised look, Wilhelmina gave a knowing smile and added: "But Mom, I am a gurl."

It was my son's birthday and my rush to get home was interfering with the visit. As Wilhelmina spoke, and then paused for a long time, I was thinking of her childhood and Micah's. He had been delivered by Dr. Romance. As a toddler, Micah was a terrible flirt, so it was fitting that Dr. Romance would be the one to deliver him into this world. Wilhelmina was not charming. I wonder what doctor had delivered her? There is, I noticed on the internet recently, a doctor named "Dr. Pain."

In our haste to get Micah home before Christmas, the doctor reluctantly allowed his discharge, though his weight was under six pounds.

Carolyn's brother and sister-in-law had braved a storm to visit. The very first time we changed Micah, it was on our living room couch and his uncle was positioned behind the couch, looking down. As soon as the diaper came off him, the rush of cold air stimulated a reaction and he peed a straight stream of piss right up onto his uncle's sweater.

As I remembered this in semi-darkness of the nursing home room—the uncle's shocked immobility, the amazing absorption of the sweater, the laughter of his wife, the embarrassed apology of my wife, and my thought of "Wow, that is an impressive stream"—I smirked a bit.

Wilhelmina caught the slight upturn of the corners of my mouth—not so much saw it, maybe, but sensed it.

Her story continued and it took me a second to catch the thread as it had dangled there without my attention as I thought of my very vital, very healthy son.

"Mudder knowt dat I wvood alwvays haf pain." As she said it, her mind's eye saw her own mother. "Wvat it taught me wvas to pray. We haf a powerful wveapon you know. Wve can pray."

This signalled the end of our visit. Her eyes squinted and I realized that a new pain was emerging. The meds were wearing off and the supper meds would arrive shortly.

Years later, I realized how much Wilhelmina's saying impacted me: "We have a powerful weapon. We can pray." In these words was a subtle lesson, one that took much reflection to unravel.

How unkind her mother seemed. But as a parent of grown children, I understand the power of a mother who is truthful to her young, suffering daughter. This woman of faith had told her daughter that she'd suffer, and in response this young child was raised not to complain or mourn, but to bring her needs to God.

Most touching of all, I realize, is that Wilhelmina's most frequent prayers and requests were not for herself, but for her sons, whom she loved so much. She longed that they should know the joy of a lifetime spent wielding a powerful weapon.

CAN'T HELP MYSELF

Carolyn and I realized long ago that our young children were like sponges. They picked up things we intended, but even more than that, they absorbed all kinds of things we didn't intend.

> *But you must continue to believe this truth and stand firmly in it. Don't drift away from the assurance you received when you heard the Good News.* (Colossians 1:23)

A new friend of mine, Len, is an honourable father and shining example of Christ. When I asked him about this, he noted that up to eighty-five percent of our youth drift away from God. He went to God in prayer and wrestled, not wanting to lose any of his eight children to the world.

"I want my children to be the fifteen percent that honour You," he said.

The reply of our Lord: "Be a fifteen-percent dad."

That means one who models the faith. One who has integrity. One who puts Christ first. To stand firm in the Good News is to stand against the prevailing culture of our world.

I honour you, Len. I see Christ in you and join you in prayer for your children and for all our children. May God grant our request, that we be part of the fifteen percent. May we be dads who give our all for Christ so that our children, as Psalm 112 puts it, will be mighty in the land, the generation of the upright who are blessed.

> O MERCIFUL Father, to whose house of many mansions Thy child shall one day approach alone, by lying down to sleep, let Thy renewing hands be upon me, and Thy loving eyes behold me as I go to sleep this night. Thou who givest Thy beloved sleep, grant that I may rest at peace with Thee, and with all Thy creatures. Renew my body, and cleanse my heart and soul by Thy creative power, and grant that the morning light may make me rejoice alike in rendering new service to Thee, and in being one day nearer to the vision of Thy face; for His sake, who died for us and rose again, Jesus Christ our Lord—Amen.
> —Rev. Kemper Bocock (1857–1904)

DECEMBER 23

Amaryllis

"BROWN BREAD!" HIS FACE REDDENED AGAIN AS HE SAID IT, WITH STACCATO inflection on each word. "You can't serve brown bread for communion."

If I were to keep track, this must be item 214 or 215 that they never taught me in seminary. Who cares if the communion loaf is white or brown, if it is cubed or whole, if we use a common cup or individual tiny cups? Of course, the council—the group made up of elders and deacons who take care of the church's functioning—cared endlessly about such things, and all the more since one or two congregants had complained about it.

Normally a ready answer, quip, assault, or comment is prepared to leave my tongue—and sometimes it does leave my mouth before my brain is fully engaged and the filters kick in. This time, however, I stopped myself. Divine intervention, as I look back. It could only have been divine intervention which kept me from stirring things up worse than they already were.

There are times when my soul delights in the joy of the Lord. In fact, that has been a pretty steady state for me since my late teen years. However, recently, there were more and more little pitched battles at my prairie charge. One thing here and another little nitpicking there and I was left dry, empty, and struggling.

Every Christmas, our faithful amaryllis plant would bloom. The amaryllis is like an oversized tulip bulb which is planted one third of the way into the soil. After a week or two, a small fractured green line appears next to the place on the top of the bulb where eventually leaves will sprout. That small notched line indicates that a flower is forming. The trumpet-like blooms are white, pink, or red, or have some combination of these colours. They are beautiful.

Stubbornly, this year, the plant was as barren and dry as my soul.

A flash of insight helped to diffuse the inappropriate response which otherwise might have escaped my mouth.

"In the Old Testament, at the Passover, what kind of bread was used?" I asked.

Their council members' answers came quickly. Unleavened bread. Bread made without yeast, the bread of hurried preparation. Exactly the right answer. The men of the council did know their Bible.

"Follow the thread, gentlemen," I said with as neutral a tone as I could deliver. "When Jesus celebrated the Passover, what kind of bread would He have used?"

"Unleavened bread."

"The white loaves of bread we use were not available until the 1400s. Bread was always made from the whole kernel of wheat, so inevitably it would have been whole barley or rye bread. Whatever grain and bread was common was used for the celebration throughout the centuries."

(Without ready access to the internet searches and online encyclopaedias we have today, I had to make up the century on the fly, but I was somewhat convinced of its accuracy, since I love reading historical novels. Somewhere in the last few months of reading, one of my books had made a big deal of the white bread presented to guests.)

Silence followed.

One of the leaders of the council noted, "It would have been better for you to announce this and prepare the congregation for the brown bread rather than just celebrate the Lord's Supper with unfamiliar bread."

For *once*, I offered a meek nod for once.

Surely it would have been inappropriate to throw the custodian under the bus. He was always so organized and prepared. Every time the members of church celebrated the Lord's Supper, he'd make sure there was enough bread, that the tiny little cups had been poured and prepared, and the table spread with a beautiful white linen cloth. This one Sunday, out of all the Sundays in all the years, there had been a glitch.

On Saturday afternoon, unexpectedly, one of the custodian's sons came home for a visit. It was natural to offer a meal. Since Saturdays were usually quite casual, no dinner had been prepared and naturally Mom pulled a loaf of bread out of the freezer. The meal was great and a joy. It was true communion.

On Sunday morning, to his horror, the custodian noted the only bread left in his freezer was brown bread. The loaf designed for the celebration of the Lord's Supper had been consumed the night before.

Urgently, penitently, he called me. "Should I go out and buy bread on Sunday and risk being seen in a store on Sunday or should I use this loaf of brown bread?"

He was serious.

A second's reflection jolted me to the awareness that the legalism of some of our members would certainly lead to great troubles later if he'd have been caught shopping for bread on Sunday.

"Use the brown loaf," I replied.

How simply the obvious decision was made and how innocent we both were of the possible consequences. Of course, hindsight is 20/20, so the fact that the custodian was calling me in a bit of a panic should have alerted me to the potential scuffle I would have with the council over this issue. It was mine to take on the chin. This custodian was a keeper and his elders and deacons should not have been sniffing around him, fault-finding, when they were already so inclined to underpay him for the work no one else wanted to do.

Taking off my hat and gloves and finding a blanket on the floor next to the couch, I sank into the couch with the blanket wrapped around me. The TV didn't interest me. For the next few minutes, all I wanted was some silence and a chance to empty my mind of the strange, petty arguments which had peppered the meeting. Carolyn, discreetly taking her cue from my silence, nodded and quietly said, "It was a tough meeting, I guess. I'm going to bed. Don't stay up too late. Don't worry about it."

The house settled into quiet. I was unhappy with the efforts to clear my mind and realized I was getting irritated with one or two of the men who should have known better. It seemed that the very people who were supposed to be supportive were always looking for the next little battle, the next little thing which needed to be corrected, rather than looking for ways to cast vision, instead of looking for ways to build the church.

Now I realized what an appropriate leader I was, in my mind: picking battles with each of them and fault-finding those I considered to be the chief culprits. Twenty years later, I can think of two who seemed to pick at every little thing.

Forgiveness. Only forgiveness allows a team to be honest, face grievances, answer the constituency, and forge the way forward.

Standing up, I shrugged off the blanket. Not really sure of what I wanted to do, I went to my study. Nope. Didn't want to read. When I saw the prayer corner, I realized that I wasn't able to pray.

I wandered into the kitchen. The cold floor dissuaded me from fixing a snack. Knowing that the cold blew mercilessly into the house via the cracked caulking of the sliding doors in our small dining room, I stepped into the dining room to draw the curtains. The theory was that the dancing curtains might restrain some of the cold from penetrating the rest of the house.

Turning from the task of drawing the curtains, my eyes happened to glance at the amaryllis plant. I examined it closely. The huge bulb rose up from the dry soil, and there, right where the leaves would start, was the first notched line of the flower. It was weeks past the usual flowering time. But it was a sign of life, a moment of great hope. In a few weeks' time, a large red flower would unfurl and the centre of each trumpet would bloom white. My soul sang, "Blessed be the Lord who rescues His people and brings His deliverance."

Laughing, I decided it had been very wise not to mention at the council meeting that last year's New Year's Day communion juice hadn't been real grape juice of any kind. The grape juice had been accidently knocked off the church kitchen counter; the glass bottle shattered, and there had been no other grape juice to be acquired so close to the start of the service. All that was available in enough quantity was a dark red iced tea which was going to be used for the children's refreshments after the worship service. A few frozen cans of lemonade were defrosted and substituted for the children and the iced tea was put to good use as the communion drink du jour. Yeah, it was probably smart that I didn't mention that.

The text this day focuses our attention on the major, not minor, things of life. When Christ returns, He will judge the earth and the tiny things we wrestled with and fought about will fade to unimportance as we consider Him whose glory will fill the skies and the earth and all the universe. Perhaps even now we can focus on what is important.

Look! The L ORD is about to destroy the earth and make it a vast wasteland. He devastates the surface of the earth and scatters the people. Priests and laypeople, servants and masters, maids and mistresses, buyers and sellers, lenders and borrowers, bankers and debtors—none will be spared. The earth will be completely emptied and looted. The L ORD has spoken! …In that day the L ORD will punish the gods in the heavens and the proud rulers of the nations on earth. They will be rounded up and put in prison. They will be shut up in prison and will finally be punished. Then the glory of the moon will wane, and the brightness of the sun will fade, for the L ORD of Heaven's Armies will rule on Mount Zion. He will rule in great glory in Jerusalem, in the sight of all the leaders of his people.
(Isaiah 24:1–3, 21–23)

In the movie *The Best Exotic Marigold Hotel*, the main character, Sonny, is a young man in India who is trying to resurrect an old hotel. He faces seemingly insurmountable odds. His favourite phrase seems to be, "Everything will be all right in the end. So if it is not all right, then it is not yet the end."

Isaiah laments with the people, crying out that things are not all right. Nations are acting without justice, the rich oppress the poor, kindness seems foreign, and food and medicines are hoarded from those who need it. Petty rulers claim to be gods and act like demons, slaughtering the innocents. The promise is that everything will be all right in the end. The Lord of Heaven's Armies will arise, and He will put everything right; there will be a new heaven and new earth and He will reign in the New Jerusalem and the new world will be just, joyful, loving, and wondrous. The same God who created heaven and earth, who sent us the Saviour Jesus Christ, is the one who is making all things all right, all new.

Be my vision, O Christ my King. Fill my thoughts and my heart with the awareness of the ever nearer approaching of the New Jerusalem and the great joy it will bring. When the ordinary things of my day threaten to distract and overwhelm me, renew in me the expectation of the soon-to-be extraordinary day of Your glorious return. Amen.

DECEMBER 24

Home-Schooled

ONE OF THE COUPLES WE OCCASIONALLY VISITED WITH HAD A FARM. IT WAS always a treat for our children to go there as there were cows to see and teats to laugh at. Even the word "teats" poked their juvenile minds to the point of laughter; the stoic way in which the farm kids could say "teat" and not even chuckle added to the hilarity. There were chickens scratching around, pigeons all the over the place, and barn kittens to be chased, caught, and carefully held. The hayloft had great places for jumping, and the odd scurrying mouse didn't bother the family's girls at all, so our boys realized there was nothing to fear in their presence at all.

Joshua, the middle son of this family, always seemed to have a mess of questions for us. "Does the traffic keep you awake at night?" Then, before we could answer, "Do the streetlights come on at the same time? Can you turn them off? What if they shine exactly into your bedroom and your curtains don't block the light? Can you turn them off then?"

The farm was nestled in a particularly bucolic setting between rolling hills and valleys, shielded from city lights. It afforded deep, dark nights that were a perfect backdrop for stunning displays of northern lights. What a joy it was to see those. The moonlit nights were eerily bright as the snow reflected the light of the moon.

The family was inquisitive because of the great training they had received as home-schooled youth. All questions were encouraged by the parents, who expected the children to write paragraphs about any and all new experiences. Visitors were a great source for new journal entries, though I often wondered how accurate those might actually be since I cannot ever recall seeing any of the little tykes taking notes.

Carolyn was particularly the target for this young lad's questions. Joshua's underlying curiosity about what she did all day framed his questions, statements, and reflections as he tried to imagine city life. For some reason it made sense that the minister was busy in some mysterious way not quite describable, but for a woman to be home and not have a farm… what on earth could occupy her? And stranger still, what could possibly fill her day when there was no home-schooling to occupy the hours?

In order to give some relief to farm mama and some excitement to our young friend, it was decided a field trip to the city would be a great adventure. Joshua's first disappointment occurred when he realized our two young sons, just slightly younger than he was but still fun play and wrestling companions, would not be home all day; they would be attending the local Christian school. Even our daughter would be gone to her play care centre.

At breakfast, I heard the oft-repeated question aimed at Carolyn: "What do you *do* in the city all day long?"

I raised my eyebrow and Carolyn smiled slightly, nodding at my unspoken inquiry. She was going to show our friend what a regular day looked like in town.

First there were the breakfast dishes to clear up. (We didn't have a dishwasher yet.) That in itself turned out to be a funny story. The dishes had to be cleared, washed, dried, and put away before the children were dressed and made ready for school. Then Carolyn drove the boys off to school. Later I heard that our little friend, Joshua, gave a dispirited wave as he realized again that he would not be joining them for this adventure. I mean, there was an ice rink at the school and a huge hill which had all kinds of kids sliding down piled high on their toboggans and sleds.

They were barely home for a breather and then were off again. Elayna needed to be brought to her play care. They had a chance to go in and see the vast array of toys, blocks, and books and the huge craft area. For a kid used to finding things to do and ways to amuse himself, this was a veritable funhouse, a riotous place of learning. But he had to go home—that is, the field-trip home—and learn more about city life.

Ever a stickler for her routines, Carolyn had her young helper make the beds. The sidewalks needed to be shovelled, not that it had snowed again, but the prevailing winds had partially covered the walkway and the mail carrier wouldn't come up to the house if the passage was so snowy. Then the toy room downstairs needed to be straightened up. Then the laundry, including endless loads and piles and folding and sorting, needed attention.

Joshua knew all about laundry. Our young farm guest happily tattled on his mom, telling us that his family's laundered clothes often stayed unfolded in the laundry baskets for days on end. They'd get in the way of people passing through the kitchen on their way outside. His mom would put them up on chairs so the baskets of clean clothes wouldn't get in the way, then she'd put them on the floor for meal times—and put them back on the chairs when the meals were done. He reported this could go on for two or three days at a time.

Oh yes, he knew all about laundry.

Carolyn nodded sharply in the direction of the clothes he was helping her to fold.

Lunch provided a leisurely break with some fun treats. Before Carolyn had married me, she was a baker by trade and she had maintained these skills. When we had special company, such as our young farm lad, she would bring out something like *boterkoek* (a Dutch treat, something like a buttery rich almond shortbread that's more cake-like in texture).

Once lunch was complete, the dishes needed to be done. Then a bit more baking while early preparations for supper could be made. Joshua almost yelped with surprise when he saw the small pan needed for potatoes. At his house, every supper no doubt consisted of a great vat of cooked potatoes; this little handful wouldn't even make his daddy happy, let alone the older brothers and sisters and the rest of the family.

Joshua laughed to himself. He was an expert potato peeler. While idly chatting, he gave away more than he probably realized. He confided to Carolyn, "If'n we're bad, we has to peel taters for Mom." It was clear from the paper-thin skins that rolled off the potatoes in quick, unbroken lines that this little kid spent lots of time peeling.

By the time Elayna was picked up from play care and Adrian and Micah from school, it was apparent that our little friend had had a very full day. He was thrilled to see the boys and be released from the duties of setting table. He ran downstairs to undo all the clean-up which the morning had required.

A few days later he returned home with his journal tucked under his arm, the entries privately prepared and off-limits to Carolyn and me. We got out of the van as he gave a half-skip, preparing to run into his house. Suddenly he leaned with arms flapping to prevent his fall. Joshua wheeled, changed direction, and instead ran towards Carolyn. He gave her a big hug, with great abandon and gratitude, and squeezed probably a bit tighter than he intended. He stepped back, and just before turning away, furrowed his brow as he sought exactly the right words. "You really are busy in the city, Mrs. V."

It was the greatest compliment this little one could offer. And it was touching. Carolyn often complained to me, "What have I really accomplished in this day?" My response was inevitably, "The children are loved, fed, cared for, and you enable me to carry out my duties. I can't do what I do without you!"

This little lad's hug and words proved to be an exclamation of timely affirmation.

Faithful service to Jesus, our Saviour and Lord, includes the work of the missionary who goes to far-flung places and the work of a parent at home who faithfully cares for the needs of a growing family and does so in Jesus' Name.

And all the people who belong to this world worshiped the beast. They are the ones whose names were not written in the Book of Life that belongs to the Lamb who was slaughtered before the world was made.

Anyone with ears to hear should listen and understand.
Anyone who is destined for prison will be taken to prison.
Anyone destined to die by the sword will die by the sword.
This means that God's holy people must endure persecution patiently and remain faithful. (Revelation 13:8–10)

Prayer. Fasting. Bible reading. Those who wish to endure persecution will wean themselves from the things which this world celebrates, joining together instead to hold on to God. The Lamb does not allow dual citizenship: a person's name is either written in the Book of Life, and such a person lives unconditionally for the glory of God by the power of His Spirit, or that person is a citizen of the world and lives blaspheming God.

> O GOD, who art the Author of Peace and Lover of concord, in knowledge of whom standeth our eternal life, whose service is perfect freedom; defend us, Thy humble servants in all assaults of our enemies, that we, surely trusting in Thy defence, may not fear the power of any adversaries, through the might of Jesus Christ our Lord—Amen.
> —Gelasian Sacramentary, 494 A.D.

DECEMBER 25

Non-Smoker

So the Word became human and made his home among us. He was full of unfailing love and faithfulness. And we have seen his glory, the glory of the Father's one and only Son. (John 1:14)

Sin is no longer your master… Instead, you live under the freedom of God's grace. (Romans 6:14)

WHAT FIRST DREW ME TO LOOK AT ABE'S HANDS WAS THE LONG UNCUT NAIL ON his middle finger. The thick nail had a curve in it. Looking at it casually so as not to get caught staring, I wondered how hard this nail must have been to cut. In the back of my mind, a quiet voice chuckled: *Ha, it'd be hard as nails to cut.* The small quiver of a smile that touched my lips got his attention and I had to focus back on our card game.

Then, as Abe held his cards across the table from me, a flash of the deeply absorbed yellow nicotine stains caught my eyes. Even his ring finger was yellowed—by association with the other two, I guess.

In those days, I was still a smoker as well. Since I wasn't allowed to savour the long pull of a cigarette while playing cards in the living room, my elderly friend and I were banished to the front porch, even in the cold blast of a blustery winter night. Once in a while Carolyn would have compassion on us (more likely compassion on our friend's advancing age and the fact that the front steps were not as well-shovelled as they should have been). At such times, she'd deign to allow us to smoke in my study, which was across the hall from the living room. The window had to be cranked open, so it was still skin-prickly cold.

As Abe flicked ash all over my desk, in the general direction of the ashtray, he'd point the cigarette and the fingers holding it at my chin and declare, "I will die a non-smoker." Yessiree, he was going to be smoke-free. Of course, in view of his advancing age, I guessed time was running out for him to implement the various schemes, plans, and cessation steps he'd accumulated. I smiled politely and avoided getting a cigarette burn on my chin as I tried to sweep live ash from the thick carpet. I always feared some lingering spark would ignite the house in the night. So his "I'm gonna quit" rant only earned my partial attention.

A phone call came an hour before our Christmas morning church service was supposed to begin. It was Abe's wife, Tina.

Abe had gotten up on time and finished his first-thing-in-the-morning-catching-up-his-nicotine-levels cigarette. He delighted in a long slow pull while savouring a mighty strong brew of coffee. I imagine that the tiny dash of cream he splashed into his mug stood straight up on the surface, unable or unwilling to take the plunge into the evil brew.

He then clutched his chest and sputtered. It was so out of the ordinary that Tina, from the living room, turned and looked at her husband. Something was seriously wrong. First she called 911. Then the minister was summoned.

I arrived just in time to see him wedged between the sink cupboard, the garbage bin, and some debris on the floor. While dabbing out his cigarette, massaging his exploding chest, and wheezing, he had thought to himself that the house wasn't quite clean enough to admit the paramedics; he tried to carry the overflowing ashtray to the kitchen so it could be dumped out. It took more concentration and coordination than he had and he went down.

Splashed over and around him was a vile mix of coffee and ashes. It made extracting him a little more difficult for the paramedics. Just before they arrived, I whispered a prayer with this elderly, frightened couple and then got out of the way to make room for the professionals to assess what was going on.

Christmas morning worship was a mix of beautiful songs sung out in full voice by the congregation filling the sanctuary. It was like they were prayers that Immanuel, God with us, would be merciful to one of our oldest attending members as he struggling in the emergency room. Awkward, shuffling silences filled the spaces between elements of the service.

As the pastor, I'd been somewhat alarmed by the sudden phone call, quick visit, and lack of opportunity to address one or two of the finer points of liturgy which would have allowed the service to flow smoothly without small interruptions. Yet those little pauses and silences impacted all of us. The third stanza of "Joy to the World" ended: "He comes to make His blessings flow far as the curse is found." Ach, the curse of sickness. Ach, the curse of getting old. Ach, living God, bring Your healing.

It was about a week before I got to see my friend in the hospital by himself. The ICU was always filled with doctors and nurses and orderlies bringing meals or clearing trays. Family members visited from far-flung corners of the province, risking the bitter cold and deep snows in order to see their beloved uncle, grandpa, and brother.

As I stepped off the elevator, Abe had been alone long enough to really want a good jaw. His sightline went straight to the elevator, and as soon as the door opened and he recognized me, he motioned with a crooked index finger. It was so filled with fluid that it looked bigger than a barbequed hotdog. He motioned again for me to come close, quickly.

In the few seconds it took to approach him, I noticed a wide variety of things. His right arm had the IV with strange liquids mixing together and flowing into him. He had pads and patches where he'd fallen, bumped his head, and scraped his hands in the kitchen. On the other side of him was a thick black pressure cuff armband and a wide tube that pumped the air in and out. There were so many monitor cords and unidentifiable-to-laypersons medical thingies that he looked like he was bound to the bed. The bedpan on his right, near his knee, confirmed that he wasn't getting out of bed anytime soon.

As I got closer, I could see that the yellow on the index finger hadn't faded at all.

Impatiently, he moved the oxygen mask a little lower to his chin so he could be heard more clearly, having lately realized that the flow of air and the mask muffled his speech and made him less comprehensible. Still, he was tough to understand. I leaned in close.

"Guess what, dominee?" Abe triumphantly intoned.

I couldn't imagine.

Hacking a bit, he said, "I've been a non-smoker for seven days now!" Unmistakeable pride and joy fought against the wheezes and phlegm in his voice. "Ya, de plans are coming good. If this keeps up I'm going to totally quit smoking. I will die a non-smoker."

"Um, cool." It was all I could manage without bursting out laughing. Of course he was a non-smoker. Helga the Strong, who patrolled the ward, wouldn't even let him up to pee. What were the odds he was going to make it down three floors and across the atrium to the outdoor smokers' section? Yet I looked again and realized he was really pleased about this. For him, missing Christmas celebrations and the annual New Year's Eve parties paled in comparison to this good news: he'd not had a cigarette in seven days.

The last conversation I ever had with him was exactly seven days later. He asked me, "Have you prayed for me?" Before the near indignant "Yes, Abe, of course!" passed my lips, he continued: "Have you prayed for me about quitting smoking?"

He laid back down.

"I'm going to meet Jesus as a non-smoker," he said serenely. "I haven't had a cigarette in more than two weeks."

It was his final, proud accomplishment. A hard worker. A labourer. A family man. A devoted husband. A card-player (okay, a get-away-with-cheating-if-I-can card player). A grandfather. A believer who finally felt fit to meet his Saviour and declare, "I'm finally a non-smoker." It'd never be engraved on his grave-marker. It'd never be declared at all to others, as no one else really knew this urgent desire he had harboured for long ago. His friends and family had given up any hope of his quitting.

The phone call came from Tina a few hours later: "Pastor, he died."

I knew there was a celebration in heaven. One redeemed sinner, a recent victor over cigarettes, a new non-smoker, had finally lifted his eyes and arms to the Saviour who had answered his prayers and now received him.

Joy to the World!

Joy to the world! the Lord is come:
let earth receive her King.
Let every heart prepare Him room,
and heaven and nature sing,
and heaven and nature sing,
and heaven, and heaven, and nature sing.
No more let sin and sorrow grow
nor thorns infest the ground.
He comes to make His blessings flow,
far as the curse is found,
far as the curse is found,
far as, far as the curse is found.
When You return dear Jesus, O Blessed One,
may You find all things ready,
and Your servants waiting for no new master,
but for one long loved and known.
Even so Maranatha, come quickly, Lord Jesus Christ.
—Updated and adapted from *A Book of Simple Prayers*, 1877

DECEMBER 26

Gifted

THE CHRISTMAS MUSIC IN THE MALL WAS BEGINNING TO SOUND TINNY AND TIRED. Shoppers had lined up for hours in order to get in on the Best Boxing Day Sales Ever event. Hard to believe that just the day before it had been a highlight to sing the great carols and hymns of the Incarnation with inspired awe. Our congregation had braved the cold to attend the annual Christmas morning worship service. The candles glowed beautifully against the frosted panes of glass obscuring the winter landscape outside and making opaque mirrors.

The little congregation had sung with full gusto. Talented and not-so-talented children gave their performances, waved their fingers to adoring grandparents, and avoided the furrowed-brow frowns of helicopter parents who wanted their little Jonny or Jane to perform to perfection.

It was interesting, though, because the pews had noticeable gaps, places where the usually faithful had skipped the service in order to sleep in, to open gifts, and as one congregant, Grandma Pietje, informed me, "to lounge all day in sleepwear that consisted of footie pyjamas."

What distracted me was seeing Pietje at the mall, casually dressed in an outlandish tracksuit, wallet in one hand while the rest of her body was advantageously angled so the other could reach deep into the fifty-percent-off bin for the latest movie-based space toys. I nodded my hello and heard no reply beyond the grunt of stretching and reaching to grasp that final component which would complete the set.

Grandma Pietje had done her level best to please all the grandkids. There had been wish-lists and spending limits, and various grandchildren had whispered additions in Grandma's ear (so that anxious parents would not be upset at the greed such wish-lists seemed to inspire in their progeny).

It would be the first year Grandpa wasn't there. It seemed something needed to be done to fill the terrible space, the empty chair, the extra helping of food which no one would eat, like the plate of his favourite cookies, the ones with the coconut which no other family member could ever gag down. But Grandpa would eat three or four at a time, when he figured Grandma wasn't looking and his diabetes numbers weren't too high.

It was a cat-and-mouse game of love between Grandpa and Grandma. The very person who scolded him for eating wrong and overindulging in sweets was the same one who baked his favourite coconut concoction cookies.

He always knew what to get the kids. He'd have his eyes open in October already and scoop up a particular block set for their grandson, Adam, who was obsessed with toys based on the latest series of movies about aliens or space creatures. There'd be the caterpillar book that no one else had seen at the bookstore; it had great information, tactile strips, and pages that could be coloured in. In the age before limitless information and misinformation on the internet, this kind of book was considered child-friendly, cutting-edge, and educational. A felicitous combination. Little Sassafras, Grandpa's nickname of endearment for the information miner, would squeal in delight to learn more about bugs and add to her considerable library of lightning bugs and books distinguishing moths from butterflies, and now a book on identifying caterpillars.

Grandma could name a favourite dish and dessert of each child, child-in-law, child-in-law wannabes, and all the grandkids. But she could not get the right gift, no matter what.

Sassafras had made Grandma so insecure this year. When the space set was being opened by her brother Adam, he managed to seem pleased enough to make Grandma satisfied. But Sassy piped up, "That's the wrong set. It's last year's movie and the pieces on this one aren't nearly as nice as this year's movie game pieces."

Parents shuddered. With the little spaceship frozen in mid-air, Adam, wide-eyed and mouth hanging open, paused briefly. "Grandma, this one is good enough," he yammered. "How would you know what us kids play with?" Adam hunched his shoulders as he realized he was doing his best to console his grandma, but for some reason he couldn't quite understand, his words only made her feel worse.

Behind her eyeglasses, which looked like giant glass coasters, Grandma's eyes got a faraway look. She was thinking how she'd make this right. Taking aside her son and daughter-in-law, and speaking low in the kitchen so that other children and grandchildren wouldn't overhear, she shared the plan she'd suddenly hatched. Sassy and Adam would come for lunch tomorrow.

"Just the two of them," she said. "Make sure they're hungry. I'm going to make this right."

Over the protests of the two standing in front of her, Grandma insisted on having her way. Which is why she was rooting around in the bargain bin.

Clutching her prize, she managed to get to a till and pay for the gift. Then, as her car slid along the deeply grooved snow ruts of the unploughed streets, Grandma reviewed the recipe for the mini-pancakes the grandkids loved so much. That would be the treat, having the pancakes for lunch. She had just the pan for them, imported from the Netherlands, which could cook nine at a time. Then they'd open the gift. The right gift. The gift she should have given to begin with if only she'd listened better, or knew whatever movie was current.

It worked out perfectly. At least, it seemed perfect. The mini-pancakes were done just as the grandkids came up the walkway. The neighbour boy had cleared the snow and was so pleased to get an extra generous tip for getting there early in the morning, freeing Grandma to get to the Best Ever Boxing Day Sale on time.

It was hard to gauge how much to let the kids eat. Those little pancakes slid down so easily. There'd be icing sugar on one, honey and cinnamon on the second, banana and chocolate chips and syrup on the third. With great enthusiasm they ate, laughed, and sensed that Grandma was trying her best to make up for something, something they couldn't quite understand. But who cared? They were eating their favourite mini-pancakes.

Finally, both shoved their plates away and Sassy and brother Adam reached for their glasses of milk. They brought it to their lips… and set it down, untasted. They were too full even to add a sip of milk, milk which might have washed the cloying sweetness from their teeth and gums and tongue. A sweetness which gained an odd potency even though they weren't adding another bite.

It was the first time Grandma ever let them leave the table without clearing their plates, cutlery, and glasses. The table remained a mess. Woo-hoo! A new grandma, a new freedom.

She took Sassy and Adam by the hand, even though they were way, way too old for this sort of thing—except when it was close to bedtime and they were tired and it was time to snuggle and read. She brought them to the Christmas tree, Adam moving slowly and Sassy skipping along. All the gifts were gone, and the dusting of needles around the edge of the tree skirt indicated that it was time, past time, to pull that old wreck down.

There was still one gift under the tree, though. It had a tag on it, reading "Adam."

Using Grandpa's nickname, which was only now beginning to feel appropriate for her to speak out loud, Grandma said, "Sassy, your favourite meal in the world is mini-pancakes, so you have received that as another gift from me." She smiled a tight smile and turned to Adam. "Here is the corrected gift from me."

Her smile relaxed and broadened, but still carried a hint of anxious anticipation; the eyebrows gave it away. She nodded to him, encouraging him to open the gift.

Now Adam's movements slowed even more. He was conserving energy, or maybe the day had been a strain on him and he felt overwhelmed. Grandma wasn't in a noticing mood at the moment; she just wanted to fix the error she'd made.

Adam tore the last of the wrapping away and his grin and flash of appreciation turned on a dime. Something was wrong. Panic now filled his eyes. Dropping the gift, his hands flew to him mouth.

It all happened in slow motion for Grandma. She'd just begun to really enjoy his pleasure, and her mind wasn't nimble in picking up what was going on. Time seemed to be exaggerated as the maternal instincts began to fight to the front of her brain. This kid would need something, fast.

His stomach began rippling. Pulling inwards, his shoulders heaved and shook—and suddenly there it was, a mighty volume of vomit projecting, spilling, and flowing all over the edge of the tree, covering his gift and seeping through his open fingers onto his jeans and into his sweater.

"Adam is barfing," Sassafras shrieked. "Grandma! Adam. Is. Barfing."

It was like time jumped to its regular speed at the second invocation of the dreadful word: barfing.

Grandma sighed, acknowledging that the freshly deep-cleaned carpets were going to need another round of cleaning. The tree was now done for the season and would somehow need to be hauled out without vomit detaching as it moved through the house to the curb. Grandma upended the big bowl, which had a few walnuts left in it from the day before. She put it under Adam's chin. The fountain kept flowing, but for the most part it stayed in the bowl.

She guided him expertly to the bathroom and lifted the toilet seat for him. As he let loose the final volleys, she started running the bathwater. Normally he was way too old for Grandma to help him with this, but when he was this sick he welcomed any nurturing, any attention, anything that would make the hurting stop.

By the time it was all over, Grandma had cleaned as much as possible. She then drove Sassafras and Adam home.

The plastic had kept the toy pieces from getting dirty, but the cardboard backing had suffered the double indignity of getting soiled and then soaked with a warm, soapy sponge. It was enough of a reminder that Adam couldn't hold it in his hand, for fear of unleashing his stomach one more time. Ever practical, Grandma wrapped the toys in a plastic bag and set them on the seat beside her for later.

Mom and Dad gingerly hugged Adam, kissed Sassafras, and turned on the latest kids' video. Something about animated dinosaurs solving some crisis or other. Dad set coffee. Mom got the laundry started. Grandma picked up the toys and walked over to Adam's closet. As she opened it, out fell exactly the same toys she'd gone out for so early that morning. Still wrapped in their plastic casing, with a firm and dry cardboard backing. Her mouth set in a firm line. She didn't know what to make of all these Christmas shenanigans.

Then Grandma's eyes rested on Adam's bedside table. There was the picture Bible Grandpa had given Adam for his last birthday. It was his favourite one. And its pages were opened to the story of Jesus' birth—the story they read every single year around the family table after eating a wonderful Christmas feast. The rush of Christmas planning, the grief of loss, and the tumult of hearts had somehow overshadowed the story this year. For the first time in memory, they had not read together the Good News of great joy that is for all the people. And it was the year they had needed it most.

Boxing Day can show us our skewed priorities. What seemed so important and precious before quickly loses its appeal. (Photo by Michelle D. VanderSpek)

> *I hate all your show and pretense—the hypocrisy of your religious festivals and solemn assemblies... Away with your noisy hymns of praise! I will not listen to the music of your harps. Instead, I want to see a mighty flood of justice, an endless river of righteous living... You drink wine by the bowlful and perfume yourselves with fragrant lotions. You care nothing about the ruin of your nation.* (Amos 5:21, 23–24, 6:6)

It's strange. In the name of Christmas, partygoers get drunk and exchange dollar-store gifts and meaningless intimacies. Secular singers prostitute themselves by singing new arrangements of sacred songs and carols—all for a special Christmas price. Credit cards are rung up to ruin, and for so many people January is a hellish balancing act of trying to make payments.

We were made for something so much bigger. We were created to worship the living God. We were formed in order to bring justice to a world gone mad with the latest scandal, addicted to pornography, numb from things that will never satisfy, and awash in anger and hopelessness.

> *For unto us a child is born, unto us a son is given: and the government shall be upon his shoulder: and his name shall be called Wonderful, Counsellor, the mighty God, the everlasting Father, the Prince of Peace.* (Isaiah 9:6, KJV)

This Christ-child, now our King, calls us to live justly. He, as our King and Saviour, rightfully demands that we live for a purpose greater than ourselves—and in so doing our lives are filled with work, wonder, and hope. We gladly suffer so that Jesus' justice and good government will rain down on this earth.

Hear us, O Christ, once a Child and now our King. From our useless ways of living, deliver us. Prepare us to live for Your great purposes. Give us a vision of Your glory, the Kingdom of Heaven which is breaking into our world right now. Grant us spiritual gladness and add to this Your serene peace, no matter what our earthly circumstances. Remind us that You are making us suitable for an eternity in the new heavens and new earth where Your glory will fill our days with wonders too great to describe. In the strength of Your Spirit—in my heart, in my mind, in what I do, and what I choose not to do—be glorified, Lord Jesus Christ. In the power of Your Spirit—in our hearts, in our minds, in what we do, and what we choose not to do—be glorified, Lord Jesus Christ, so that the Father's great purpose in sending You to this earth will be revealed and our shouts and praises will ring all the louder. Hallelujah! Amen.

DECEMBER 27

Lonely

IN BETWEEN CHRISTMAS AND NEW YEAR'S THERE IS A SUNDAY, AND ACCORDING to the Common Lectionary (pre-selected readings of the Bible assigned to each Sunday of the year and used by a wide variety of Christian denominations) the key passage for that day is one of weeping and lament—Rachel weeping over her children who are no more. They were swept away into exile in the Old Testament. The New Testament refers to the slaughter of the innocents, the infant baby boys up to two years old who were killed by wicked King Herod, who wanted to kill all these children in hopes of killing the newborn King. When God breaks into our world, the hosts of hell stir up trouble and chaos, trying to obscure what is unstoppable—the grace of God.

Many people who populate the pews year in and year out are used to the story and it doesn't impact them at all. They usually just want something "happy clappy," something that will extend the fairy-tale picture of Christmas that their own hearts want to keep.

Just as the service was beginning, Randolph slipped in. He wanted a place in the back, somewhere in an inconspicuous corner, but it was not to be. The back was filled. The nearest open spot was next to Vera's family, and he offered a brief shake of his head. The usher brought him three-quarters of the way to the front. It was like all the people had hunched up in the back of the church because there was something toxic about the front. Kind of like my college math class, where all the students studiously avoided the first two rows because the professor wandered around excitedly as he taught—and the greater his passion, the more spit accompanied his volley of words. Three of us had often joked about bringing umbrellas and simultaneously opening them when the spit-rain started. All that flashed through my brain briefly as he sat down. Though the pulpit was set far back from the pews, I made a mental note not to so emphasize my words that I would spit. My smile was a bit more natural. Randolph nodded; it was more than a social nod and I realized he was going to want to speak with me later.

After all the congregants had filed past and offered their greetings, encouragements, and whatever corrections they needed, I saw that Randolph had waited. He stood by himself. A congregation that had prayed, longed for, and wanted new members didn't want them to arrive on such an inconvenient Sunday, when the holidays were still in full swing and many had family and friends visiting.

Randolph marched up to me. He wanted to speak and it wouldn't wait until a more convenient time. We sat down again together in the sanctuary. It was deserted.

"I was mad at you."

That was his start and I didn't think it was too encouraging, but his hazel-brown eyes and bushy brows gave off signs that laughter and tears weren't too far off. I prepared to listen.

"Vera is mad at me," he continued. A display of genuine grief rose up. It swept across his features and drained away. Something had happened between them and it pained him, but he wasn't going to stay on this tangential topic right now. "Just after we talked, I decided I didn't want anything to do with your Jesus."

Now he had my full attention. He told the story, described how a school buddy, a casual friend, had taken him out for a drink. This friend had started talking. Paying for drinks. Waiting until the other guys they knew had left the pub. They were in an oversized booth. It was suddenly intimate, shielded from the rest of the place. It seemed there was an attraction between them; the drinks had broken down fears and conventions and barriers, and this friend invited himself back to Randolph's dorm room.

Randolph thought maybe this friend had invited himself under the pretence of giving the slightly drunk Randolph a safe way back to the dorm. The roommate was away for the weekend celebrating his parents' anniversary, so the room was free and the time all theirs.

"The kissing was good," Randolph admitted, being incredibly candid. "That would have been enough, but then his body was responding." He broke from his staccato narration and asked, raising his eyebrows and blinking his hazel-brown eyes. "You know what I mean, right? *Responding?*"

Randolph continued the story, realizing that they'd crossed a point of no return. Now Randolph was getting nervous. He was in uncharted territory. As he told the story, a hint of colour touched his cheeks. His eyes averted and he stared intently at the corner above the sound booth.

"Clothes started being pulled off," he said. They were naked, both of them at this point. Suddenly Randolph looked directly at me. "A twig and berries."

He laughed a thin, strained laugh and shook his head at the memory, blushing deeply as if he felt naked in the retelling. Tears began to form.

He addressed the comments to me directly, willing me to understand. "We don't have parts that are meant to go together. Men, I mean. At that moment, naked, I first said it softly to myself—we don't have parts that are meant to go together—as if this was the first time I realized it. And when I repeated it louder, my buddy thought I was insulting him and laughing at him."

Randolph narrated what happened next, with little hiccups catching his voice, the ones that tears can induce. This buddy threw a punch in Randolph's general direction. He missed. Now enraged, he kicked over his chair, knocked over a shelf of books, and kicked the door a few times before slamming it. Standing in the hallway, the man tried to open it, maybe to slam it again, but it was locked. So he left.

At school it was told that Randolph had made the moves on him, as if he hadn't wanted it.

"I've been thrown out of our circle of friends," he said. "It is lonely. Not one of them will speak to me."

In confusion, and with a small hope of help, he went home.

"I told my parents and they told me not to visit anymore, to just stay at the dorm." It seemed that every support was being knocked out from his life. "But the house was open over Christmas break."

It took me a second to catch up to him.

"There really isn't anyone there at the dorms," he continued. "Just a few foreign students who stick together, and the kitchen staff at the small dining hall who are ticked they have to keep meals going through the holidays. I am all alone. Vera won't speak with me. She heard the rumours first and thought I should have talked to her. She wanted to fix me, or maybe to be my friend while I was broken. Now, while everything is a mess, her mom answered the phone when I called and said I'm not welcome there and Vera won't speak with me. 'Leave her alone,' she said. 'It's awkward here in church.'"

He said it all in a very flat tone. Emptied, it seemed, of tears.

I nodded to let him know that I'd caught the awkward, nonverbal exchange between Vera's family and Randolph. How odd it was that the only open place near the back of the church should have been right next to that family. Quietly, I further thought it also odd that this family, knowing Randolph's need, hadn't found a place for him. Randolph's longings were not unfamiliar to them and they'd supported Vera's friendship with him. Now he was alone.

"Pastor, here is the worst part. I'm so lonely I don't know what to do with myself."

The tears appeared again and ran past his cheeks. On the side of his face closest to me, tracks of tears zigzagged across an unshaven patch just above his jawline.

"Here's the problem: I still have these feelings." His voice dropped very low. "You know, for men. But I can't get the picture out of my brain. Twig and berries don't go with twig and berries."

The situation was funny. It was sad. It was unashamed longing.

He had decided he wouldn't explore this sex stuff. Not now. He couldn't handle all this drama, this rejection, this rejecting, this confusion. It was Rachel weeping over what could never be.

Would God break into this situation? Maybe Randolph had

experienced such chaos exactly because he'd begun to hear the knocking at the door of his heart.

"After what I did—almost did, what I still want to do, but don't want at all…" His lashes caught some of his tears, and neither of us had a Kleenex to catch the nose drips. "I am determined not to have sex for now, until I sort some things out."

I looked away, noting that he was going to rub his nose along the length of his sleeve. He needed a second of privacy.

Then his final question and summary: "Do you think Jesus is still interested in me?"

Ah, the real question had surfaced.

"I am so alone now."

What strange impressions we have of church. So often we expect it to be a social club for people who congratulate themselves on their imagined perfections. But the church, when she is functioning as she ought to, is a triage centre for the sick and a place of healing.

> *My dear children, I am writing this to you so that you will not sin. But if anyone does sin, we have an advocate who pleads our case before the Father. He is Jesus Christ, the one who is truly righteous... I am writing to you who are mature in the faith because you know Christ, who existed from the beginning. I am writing to you who are young in the faith because you have won your battle with the evil one.* (1 John 2:1, 13)

John, the disciple who knew that Jesus loved him, wrote this to the church when he was old. "Dear children," he says. He wrote so that we will not sin. He wrote to remind young believers that the Father has taken us from the kingdom of darkness and brought us to the Kingdom of the Son He loves, the Kingdom of Light. Young believers have won their battle with the evil one because the father of lies is no longer their kidnapper; the Father of love and truth is now their Father.

We are children of God. He wrote to remind mature believers of the power of Christ, who is from the beginning and will guard us until His return. Whether you're mature or new to the faith, live in the light. Live out the salvation that is already yours and live knowing that sin is already defeated by Jesus' victory, which has taken hold of your life.

> LORD, take my lips and speak through them; take my mind, and think through it; take my heart, and set it on fire.
> —W.H.H. Aitken (1841–1927)

DECEMBER 28

Dishwasher

CAROLYN GRUMBLED, WHICH IS VERY UNUSUAL FOR CAROLYN, "YOU CAN EASILY tell the building committee is composed of men only!" We'd been in our church for more than a year and the building committee had promised to help us out.

We needed whatever help the church was prepared to offer. You see, seminary was very expensive and we still had a lot to pay back on our school loans.

Our washing machine was okay, but the matching dryer had given up the ghost a long time ago. The space under the kitchen counter where the dishwasher was supposed to go remained a glaring gap which needed attention, and the building committee was going to address these needs. Perfect.

The building committee was a volunteer group in our church, comprised of three men who made sure the parsonage was in good order. It was painted, general repairs were completed, they got cost estimates for major repairs, and so on.

Carefully counting out their money, the committee realized they may have overpromised. Instead of asking which appliance was most needed, the men went with a dishwasher. At this time, we were still up to our armpits in diapers, and in the name of good environmental practices we had opted for cloth diapers. We always had gross groupings of mini-towels, facecloths, and bibs which needed laundering, so a dryer was the obvious choice, more so since it always seemed the prairie summer and fine weather for hanging out laundry only lasted three months of the year.

But the men decided a dishwasher would be more appropriate. And so a dishwasher arrived one morning.

Two of the men volunteered their time to install it. After wedging it in place, they realized they had not attached the hose. So it had to be moved out of place and the hose attached. The problem was that neither of the hoses they'd brought with them was appropriate. So they went to the hardware store. Once the hose was properly attached, the correct attachment to tighten the hose was nowhere to be found. Carolyn was enjoying this altogether too well. Her muffled giggles and guffaws added to the men's irritation, which in turn added to her levity.

At one point, our son Adrian had to be bodily removed from watching these men work.

"Wouldn't it be easier to follow the 'structions?" he asked.

It was a well-meant question. However, it was as if he'd asked if these men were truly men or not. After all, what man needed instructions? So Carolyn hustled him out of there quick as a blink.

The one-hour job the men had boastfully predicted turned into a two-and-a-half-hour job, with three trips to the hardware store. It cut into the children's naptime, so the children were cranky, the men were frustrated, and Carolyn's merriment finally faded; she was ready to boot the men out and get her household back into order and routine.

Finally, the leader of this team of two proudly declared, "It's ready to be tested. We don't need to put any soap in it or anything. We just want to see how loud it is and make sure it doesn't leak."

The water rushed in, and then a very unusual sound issued from the machine. The men looked at one another, perplexed, and sprang into action. They stopped the cycle. They opened the door. A rush of steam blocked the view for a second. When the steam cleared, the reason for the strange sound become obvious: there, in a sealed plastic pouch, was the instruction manual, the correct hose and connectors, and other small hardware pieces that might have been needed to install the dishwasher.

Unable to contain her laughter anymore, Carolyn hurried out of the room. As our bedroom door closed, peals of laughter could clearly be heard all the way down the hall and into the kitchen.

Before Adrian could triumphantly chortle, "I told you to get the instructions," I clamped my hand into his and led him out of the kitchen.

"Go find your brother Micah, and let him know the dishwasher is working," I said. Then, with as much straight-faced solemnity as I could muster, I returned to the kitchen. I stuck out my hand. "Thanks so much for the dishwasher and for installing it."

The men, looking downwards, sheepishly, limply, shook my hand and beat a hasty retreat out of the house. Somewhere in the distance, their ears were still stinging with the sound of Carolyn's near sobs of laughter.

Sometimes we can be so irritated with one another. However, we are not called to be irritated and frustrated with one another. In reality, we will all experience painful interactions with others, for our fallen humanity is not yet restored, but it is important for us all to hold onto the vision presented to us in the passages that follow.

> *The LORD is merciful and compassionate, slow to get angry and filled with unfailing love. The LORD is good to everyone. He showers compassion on all his creation... The LORD protects all those who love him, but he destroys the wicked.* (Psalm 145:8–9, 20)

> *Then the surviving Philistines will worship our God and become like a clan in Judah. The Philistines of Ekron will join my people, as the ancient Jebusites once did.* (Zechariah 9:7)

"Bring on the destruction of the wicked." That makes all kinds of sense to us. In case God isn't sure who's wicked, I'm sure many of us have a list already prepared. Yet the mercy and undeserved kindness of God flows far and wide. Thankfully, His mercy reaches us and even the most unexpected people.

The people of Israel *hated* the Philistines, who invaded them regularly, raided their cattle, and burned their crops. Yet Zechariah saw the day when in Christ, even these most despised enemies could become a brother or sister in the faith. In fact, they could become leaders in the very tribe from which Jesus descended—part of the intimate circle.

Are you ready for such mercy? Are you prepared to receive all those whom God is drawing close to Himself in Christ? Are you a barrier to their coming or are your arms open wide?

O merciful and gracious Lord, lift up our hearts to that world which is our soul's true home, and grant that with the loosing of these earthly ties, we may care more for the people and things You care about. You have chosen us to be part of the family of faith, ready to enter into the company of the blessed who now share eternal joys. May our lives here, today, reflect the order and peace of Your heavenly kingdom. In the name of Christ, the Child and King who binds together things earthly and things heavenly, we pray. Amen.

DECEMBER 29

Demons

I'D PROBABLY LEAVE IT TO THE PENTECOSTALS OR SOME OTHER GROUP OF charismatics to refer to demons and visions of evil. Don't get me wrong, I believe the Bible. I truly believe Jesus cast out demons and that our lives need to get right else we return to devastating sins. But I'd never really heard anyone describe demons, let alone the man I was about to visit.

Harry was a facts man; he was a "show me the numbers" or "tell me how it works" kind of guy. Anything he couldn't add up or hold or see... well, he'd just need to reserve judgment on such things.

The man's great girth was almost cartoonish. As I entered the room, I saw Harry's feet under his blanket form twin peaks. The blanket dropped to his ankles, then traced a steady, steep climb up to his massive gut. Beyond that, most of his features were lost, but I could make out his nose every time he exhaled. This splotched appendage would appear and disappear with each breath. It was important not to giggle; it seemed a giggle would not be very pastoral.

He sent his wife out on an errand. To me, it was obviously contrived. That should have been my first clue that something was up. He was a bit of an abrasive man, but he and his wife were devoted to one another. Of the two of them, she was the prayer warrior. Something was agitating him and he needed to confide in me while she was away.

As soon as the door closed, he turned his head towards me. "Do you believe there are demons?"

I flipped through the various possible answers. Theologically, I knew there were demons. Biblically, I knew Jesus had cast out demons. Practically speaking, I'd never seen one, but I had friends who claimed to cast demons out. Comically, I had to supress a giggle as I thought of a cartoon panel I once saw; it featured a "small appliance faith healer" who was commanding the demons to come out of vacuum cleaners.

The man wasn't really looking for an answer.

"Yeah, me neither," Harry noted. "But now I'm plagued by them. At night I realize each cigarette I have ever taken has been pulling health from me and inviting evil. As I'm about to fall asleep, I see them dancing on my chest and belly."

Rudely I imagine what it'd be like to see a parade of pitch-forked, pointed-eared, long-tailed, smoky leprechauns dancing and staring down at him from the heights of his belly. I guess this would be a terrible sight in those twilight moments between wakefulness and sleep, awakened by chest pains.

He asked me to pray with him, and quickly, before his wife returned.

It was a testimony to his faith when he said a few days later, "Thanks for praying. From that moment on, I have not been plagued by the demons."

Surely God is gracious beyond our tiny grains of faith.

The very things that plague us may well be the prompts which push us to God.

> *But as for me, I will sing about your power. Each morning I will sing with joy about your unfailing love. For you have been my refuge, a place of safety when I am in distress. O my Strength, to you I sing praises, for you, O God, are my refuge, the God who shows me unfailing love.* (Psalm 59:16–17)

It is tempting is to rehearse all kinds of wrongs and frustrations in our lives, but the psalmist chooses something significantly different. The psalmist rehearses God's power, love, and protection.

> O God, the Protector of all who trust in You, without Whom nothing is strong, without Whom nothing is holy, increase and multiply Your mercy to us, that, with You as our Ruler and Guide, we may so pass through things temporal that we finally lose not the things eternal. Grant this, O Heavenly Father, for Jesus Christ's sake, our Lord.
> —Gregorian Prayer, *The Book of Common Prayer*, 590 A.D. (adapted)

DECEMBER 30
Fractured Memory

SOMETIMES A STORY WILL SEEM SO VIVID IN MY MIND, BUT WHEN I TELL IT MY wife will look at me with the same disgusted look she has when there's a fly in her lemonade or a fleck of food detritus left on a plate after a dishwasher cycle. Obviously I've gotten it wrong.

I'm fairly sure this is a true recollection.

On New Year's Eve, we always have plans. We always have friends to either meet or invite over to our place. But this year? Well, the flu had laid us all low. I'd already preached in the evening, and I'd be required to preach again in the morning. The kids wanted to stay up, but we were so tired, on the edge of being unable to control the queasiness of our tummies and still trying to appease our children. We hit upon a brilliant solution. We'd fool the kids.

We told the boys, "Shh, keep this very quiet. We're going to pretend it's midnight at 9:00 p.m. so that Elayna can celebrate New Year's Eve with us and then be in bed on time."

Thrilled to be in on the secret, the boys were more exuberant than usual with their sister and with one another. Many boxes of chocolates and other treats for New Year's Eve were consumed by the children as Carolyn and I nursed our grumbling intestines.

Games were abandoned and quickly small juice glasses filled with liquid so the children could join us in toasting the New Year.

Micah loathed keeping a secret and had trouble buying a gift for anyone. Inevitably he'd be telling them in advance of the date, with conspiratorial excitement, how much they would like it.

As the glasses were raised for our 9:00 p.m. countdown, "Happy New Year" rang out. Micah softly, in order to assuage his sense of justice and in order to reveal a secret he was bursting to tell, added into the mix of well-wishing, "Happy Almost New Year!"

Elayna was sufficiently proud to have stayed up and was easily convinced to climb into bed without any of the usual bedtime stories.

Ever thinking ahead, Carolyn hadn't set the clocks to the correct time of 9:10 p.m. Instead she set them for 11:10. Wise woman.

After a few more rounds of games, some tickling, and some more food, the boys were so tired they were ready to believe it was midnight at 10:00. Once again juice glass toasts were proposed for God's blessing in the New Year. This time, Micah and Adrian both excitedly proclaimed, "Happy New Year!"

They were soon hustled to bed. How willingly they threw themselves on their beds. They were almost asleep before I had a chance to turn out their light. What a delight to be able to lean over and kiss Carolyn at 10:15 p.m., wish her a blessed new year, and get a wonderful night's sleep.

CAN'T HELP MYSELF

How many precious memories are associated with family times? For many families, holiday seasons can be rife with conflict and frustration and failed expectations. When we teach our children in accord with the Word of God, the lessons also impact us for good and remind us how we are called to live.

> *Throw out the mocker, and fighting goes, too. Quarrels and insults will disappear.* (Proverbs 22:10)

Our sitcom-happy culture revels in lippy children, a dad figure who's a doofus, and a mom who has smart-aleck responses to her husband's laziness and her children's rudeness. We wonder why our schoolteachers are mocked, and are surprised to learn that our children are nasty to those in authority. Yet in our living rooms and bedrooms, and every place where there's a TV, we celebrate mocking and quarrels. In contrast, we have this invitation:

> *Whoever loves a pure heart and gracious speech will have the king as a friend.* (Proverbs 22:11)

We are called to be countercultural. We are called to be friends of Jesus Christ, the King of glory, grace, and loving-kindness. We are called to offer kind speech to everyone we meet.

> Take this one, Thy happy child safely through this new day,
> Strong Father and Faithful Friend.
> Keep each little one in Thy tender care
> until the time of evening prayers.
> When:
> It is time for sleep,
> And Thy child comes again to Thy knee
> Sure of a perfect welcome,
> Sure of forgiveness for failure,
> Sure of a sweet, deep sleep,
> Safe held in Thy care.
> Take this one, Thy happy child, safely through each day and safely through each night, Strong Father and Friend.
> —John S. Hoyland (adapted)

DECEMBER 31

Prayer

IN THE PROTESTANT TRADITION, ADVENT IS CELEBRATED LEADING UP TO CHRISTMAS, and as soon as Christmas is done the candles are packed away. Though we often sing of the twelve days of Christmas, there is little understanding that these days follow, not precede, Christmas. Still, once in a while, in helping the congregation understand that we all stand in a broader Christian community and that others celebrate in different, rich ways, the worship team leaves the Advent wreath in place, with all the candles lit, until Epiphany, January 6, which is the Twelfth Day of Christmas.

In our church, where old habits from Holland haven't faded away, New Year's Eve is also a time for gathering for worship. The Christmas decorations are partially removed, but on this particular year the Advent wreath still glowed brightly. The beautiful light, the simple wreath, and removal of many decorations which had cluttered the church in the previous weeks, left the sanctuary with a warm glow. The cosy atmosphere seemed to invite intimacy.

After the scripture readings were read and familiar hymns and carols lovingly sung, family members began to recount that year's highlights—the birth of grandchildren (or even great-grandchildren) and answered prayers. Thanks be to God for the celebration of a sixtieth wedding anniversary. Cancer was defeated for one member.

The current chairperson of the church's council stood and delivered a "state of the church" address, talking about who had died, who had been baptized, who had moved away, who had been added to our membership, and who had been married.

Then the members of the church were invited to offer prayer requests. Since this service wasn't nearly as well attended as a regular Sunday morning service, it didn't take too long to receive these requests.

This year, one of the quieter members of the church, Thea, the wife of an elder, a person very involved behind the scenes but not one to stand up in church, offered her prayer request. Of her two young adult children, one was steadfastly following the Lord and the other had drifted far away.

She cleared her throat. She leaned forward and clutched the high back of the pew in front of her for support and spoke.

"My request—actually, our request, my husband and mine—is that Jesus will do whatever it takes for my son, Zeke, to know Him."

She promptly sat down. The weight of the request settled over the various people gathered there. Anything? Whatever it takes? Wow.

There's an old semi-funny, semi-true joke that pokes its head into many ministerial gatherings. It goes something like this: "Please don't pray for me that I receive patience, because patience only comes by way of enduring suffering and I'm already knee-deep in suffering." Knowingly, other ministers will smile, nod, or picture the particular parishioners who have added to their storehouse of patience.

To this day, I don't know what moved me to ask this mom publicly, "Thea, are you prepared for whatever answer Jesus brings?"

There was a pause. Was I really expecting her to answer? Was she formulating an answer? Those others who were gathered that New Year's Eve were suddenly reluctant to shout out their prayer requests, thinking the minister might follow up with a complicated question.

She stood again. I don't know how long I'd waited or if I was actually awaiting an answer.

"Yes," she declared. "Anything He needs to do to get my son's attention and bring him to faith."

No one dared to add anything else to the request. On behalf of the church, I prayed with thanks for so many rich blessings, and I cautiously offered this father and mother's ardent request for their son.

Knowing there were many others in the same circumstances, many others who had children who had wandered far and wide from the way of truth, I remembered them also before God, but this mother's particularly poignant plea echoed through the minds and hearts of many congregants. What would the New Year bring? How would God answer this brave petition? No? Not yet? Perhaps most frighteningly of all: Yes.

Zeke was a charmer who had many friends, a wide circle of acquaintances. Today, at the mere click of a button, someone can accept fifty or five hundred friends, so the meaning of the word friend is a bit lost. Long before such social platforms, having such a wide and diverse circle of friends, and the ability to meaningfully connect with each, would be a real accomplishment.

Zeke was able to do so. There'd be parties. There'd be card nights. There'd be car rallies. There'd be last-minute, late-night, desperate study sessions with a few others who'd also partied the semester away; after endless carafes of caffeine and boxes of pizza, the few would be joined at different times by well-studied nerds who offered pointers and tips on key things to pay close attention to in order to get good marks.

This young man knew the nerds well and always waved a friendly hello, where the others would more likely mock, insult, or ignore them. It was evidence of Zeke's hearty and sincere friendliness that these nerds would go to him and offer useful advice.

January didn't yield any noticeable answer to the mother's prayer.

February came and went with virtually no contact. This troubled the mom.

March was a different story. A friend called Thea to say that Zeke was acting oddly. A cousin called to say that he had inconveniently crashed on the couch because he didn't feel he could get himself home safely. Zeke hadn't been drinking or anything like that; for whatever reason, he just didn't want to leave. What a pain. Mom drove to the university to pick him up.

After being at home for a few days, Zeke's behaviour became increasingly erratic. Finally he confessed that he was getting terrible headaches. He was having more and more trouble seeing, and at night his vision was useless.

Why hadn't he said anything sooner? Why not indeed. What kid would ever want to admit to his mom this secret fear: "I think my partying is making me go blind."

The doctor, who was very booked that day, nevertheless squeezed Zeke in for an afternoon appointment, because of the mom's urgent pleading and insistence. The son reluctantly agreed to go. His ability to save face before his peers was still intact.

"I didn't really want to go to a doctor," he would say. "But Mom is forcing me. You do these things to make Mom happy and get her off your back, so she won't nag."

The doctor used more than the promised "two minutes only" his secretary had insisted on. In fact, when she came to the examination room door to remind him that there was a waiting room full of people who'd booked appointments long before, the doctor, with gentle authority, declared that she needed to ring the eye specialist, the one connected with the university hospital in town, and get an appointment for this young man that very day. The receptionist swallowed slightly and nodded. Thea went white with fear.

In a matter of hours, Zeke was on the operating table. I was called in to meet with the family and pray. The hours passed and the scheduled length of time for the surgery long passed.

Finally the specialist approached the family. "We managed to save his eyes, but whether or not he'll actually be able to see more than twenty-five percent is still up in the air. We're going to have to wait for his recovery. He is going to have to be still and have his eyes bandaged for a while."

Being so direct wasn't rudeness on his part. It was exhaustion. This emergency surgery had happened so late in the day of an already long, overbooked day. Still, the words were painful to hear.

As soon as these words were spoken, Thea looked directly at me, and I knew she was recalling her New Year's Eve prayer request. Had she prayed away his eyesight? Had she prayed curses on her son?

Two weeks and one day later, I had the chance to visit this young man with no one else around. His eyesight had indeed been saved and there were encouraging signs that more improvement was on the way.

His mom had hovered nearby and tended him so faithfully all this time, but she had not dared to ask him any probing questions.

This morning, Mom was away and he was alone. He smiled broadly when he saw me enter the hospital room.

"Zeke, my man, what happened to you?" I asked.

Without hesitation, he said, "God finally got my attention in the only way He could have that would make me listen."

The very same God who knows our rebellions listens to a mother's earnest prayer. This is God, who works all things for the good of those who love Him.

> *Yes, I will tell you of things that are entirely new, things you never heard of before. For I know so well what traitors you are. You have been rebels from birth. Yet for my own sake and for the honor of my name, I will hold back my anger and not wipe you out. I have refined you, but not as silver is refined. Rather, I have refined you in the furnace of suffering. I will rescue you for my sake—yes, for my own sake! I will not let my reputation be tarnished, and I will not share my glory with idols!* (Isaiah 48:8–11)

> *For as the waters fill the sea, the earth will be filled with an awareness of the glory of the L*ORD. (Habakkuk 2:14)

Glory. The word speaks to the weight of the living God's majesty, and His right to rule and judge the nations. The Creator is the One who redeems His people and draws them to Himself.

At Christmas time, people rush in a frenzy to family events all the while feeling empty and exhausted. We buy gifts for people who are ungrateful and whose homes are crammed with useless stuff. We feel let down that Christmas does not fulfill our expectations.

Isaiah and Habakkuk point to something far more difficult, yet vastly richer and more satisfying. Christmas is the time when the glory of God is revealed. Christmas is the time when God's love for rebels is shown in Christ. Christmas is when the Spirit of God stirs our hearts and shows us our sins.

As a people who walk in so much darkness, we need light which the world cannot offer; we need the light of Christ. Advent candles are lit to remind us of the light of Christ. We are refined by suffering.

At Christmas time, we fast in acknowledgement of our sins. At Christmas time, we mourn the wickedness of our own hearts and cry, "Lord Jesus, make room in my heart for Your return." At Christmas time, God the Father intentionally seeks out and gathers His children. He will cleanse us from our sins. He will fill our hearts with the knowledge of His glory. At Christmas time, we look forward, with the prophet Habakkuk, to the great day when the awareness of God's glory will cover this earth.

Believers—the children of God who were found by God and refined by suffering—will shout with wonder and joy at His glory revealed. Those who ignored God, ignored all signs of His love and evidences of His presence, will stand in slack-jawed awe when He is revealed and face eternal punishment.

This day, if you hear His voice, if you glimpse His glory, turn to Him. Ask a Christian friend whose walk with God you admire, "What must I do to see the glory of the Lord?"

> Eternal Light, before whom all darkness is light, and, in comparison with Whom, every other light is but darkness, may it please You to send forth Your light and Your truth, that they may lead us. Purify, we pray You, our souls from all impure imaginations, that Your most beautiful and holy image may be again renewed within us, and, by contemplating Your glorious perfections, we may feel daily improved within us that Divine similitude the perfection whereof we hope will at last make us forever happy in that full and beatific vision we aspire after. Till this most blessed day break, and the shadows fly away, let Your Spirit be continually with us, and may we feel the powerful effects of Your divine grace constantly directing and supporting our steps; that all our endeavors, throughout the whole remaining part of our lives, may serve to promote the honour and glory of Your blessed Name, through Jesus Christ our Lord.
>
> —Robert Leighton (1611–1684)